Rev.elations
from old Parish Magazines

Written by parsons 1908 - 1933

Compiled and edited by
Rosemary and Tony Jewers

Foreword by
H.R.H. The Prince Philip, Duke of Edinburgh
KG, KT, OM, GBE, AC, QSO, PC.

Larks Press in association with Rosemary & Tony Jewers

Published by Larks Press
Ordnance Farm House, Guist Bottom
Dereham NR20 5PF
01328 829207
Larks.Press@btinternet.com
www.booksatlarkspress.co.uk

in association with Rosemary and Tony Jewers
rosemaryandtony@googlemail.com

Web: www.newrevelationsbook.co.uk
e-mail: info@newrevelationsbook.co.uk

2010

Cover cartoon: Rosemary Jewers

Printed by Think Ink, 11 - 13 Philip Road, Ipswich. IP2 8BH

British Library Cataloguing-in-Publication Data
A catalogue record for this book is available
from the British Library

The producers of this book cannot guarantee the historical accuracy of any of the articles in the original magazines from which this book has been created, but they have no reason to think that there are any intentional errors.

ISBN 978-1-904006-53-4

EAN 9781904006534

Foreword

Collecting things; either aggressively by going out and looking for the chosen objects, or passively by never being able to decide to throw anything away; seems to be a human characteristic. This little book owes its origins to the latter form of collecting. The Brereton family of Massingham were evidently incapable of throwing anything away, including old editions of parish magazines.

There are certain standard features of English country life, and one of the most cherished is the Parish Magazine. A hundred years ago, a group of West Norfolk parishes decided to publish a joint magazine, and this collection of cuttings which comes from that publication is probably typical of parish magazines throughout the country. Parish news and gossip, reactions to national events, and more or less chiding comments from the vicar may not have any great literary merit - at least not sufficient to warrant making a deliberate collection of them - but there can be nothing quite like them to give a flavour of life in a country parish.

Mr and Mrs Jewers were lucky enough to inherit copies of a magazine that served some twenty-five parishes between 1908 and 1933. The events, ideas and opinions in these cuttings may no longer be topical, but they are a sort of key-hole view of life in the country during those years. It seems that passive collecting can have a value after all.

In memory of
John and Nona Brereton
and all the clergy
whose writings made this
book possible.

Contents

Acknowledgements

We would like to thank the following people and organisations for their help and assistance in the production of this book. They have all provided valuable information and/or spent much time searching for and sending historical photographs.

The Bishop of Lynn The Rt Rev. James Langstaff
The Rev. Canon Stuart Nairn
The Rev. William Howard
The Rev. Jonathan Riviere
The Rev. James Ryan
The Rev. Stephen Thorp

David C. Apps
David Burchell & David Turner (Narborough Research Group)
Fred Cooke (Castle Rising History Group)
Mary Cook
Jeanne Fox
Brian & Jan Gadd (Photos from their postcard collection)
Marianne Gascoyne
David Grimes
Maggie & Roger Haverson
Bill Lewis

King's Lynn Museums
The University of Leeds ('Liddle Collection')

Additional help and advice:
Susan Yaxley
Ewan Harrow
Paul Sharp

The Chair, Secretary and members of all the existing PCC's of the parishes who are included in this book.

INTRODUCTION

When I inherited a collection of old parish magazines from my parents, I had no idea that I was about to unearth a treasure-trove of fascinating reading.

My great-great-grandfather, Charles Brereton, became Rector of the parish of Little Massingham, Norfolk in 1820. Subsequent Breretons followed in his ecclesiastical footsteps; becoming rectors of the same village for many years. I believe it is because of this unusual continuous line of family parsons that my copies of the magazines remained intact. It was their extraordinary content that inspired me to publish this book.

The earliest magazine was printed in January 1908 when several villages launched a joint monthly issue. The last one is for 1933. Sadly, copies for 1911-1917 are missing, but the Rev. Canon Stuart Nairn of The Nar Valley Group Benefice came to the rescue. He offered the facility to copy his magazines for the missing period. This was great news as I felt it was important to include the First World War years to demonstrate the effect it had on the nation.

The purpose of this book is to reveal an authentic slice of social history between 1908-1933, quoting from articles written by parsons at the time, when reporting on social events, activities, village spirit, gossip and news, with tales of joy and sorrow, the curious and the incredible thrown in.

Some wrote with great wit and humour, some with charisma, while others did not disguise their strong views and wrote in an outspoken manner, that the clergy today would not dare even to contemplate. It was a period when the parson was effectively the head of social services, the Chief Executive Officer who looked after his parishioners in mind, body and spirit.

If there was a shortage of parish news, parsons wrote about interesting national and local historical matters, some dating back hundreds of years. A number of these articles are included.

Some parishes appear more frequently than others, because their parson wrote more interesting accounts.

Several villages featured are within the Sandringham estate and royal involvement with the residents was an important part of life for them. Some articles provide an intriguing insight into this relationship.

When a major event occurred, such as the death of the King or the outbreak of war, all parsons wrote about them and referred to local connections. For obvious reasons it was not practical to use them all, only a representative selection.

Although the magazines relate to rural life in over twenty Norfolk parishes, there were times when high prices, unrest and strikes became major issues. These would have affected virtually everyone in the country.

The original magazines were slightly larger than this book and the cost of one old penny was maintained for some time by income from adverts. Several of these have been reproduced, as have a number of old photographs that people have kindly contributed.

I have to thank my husband Tony for his selection and editing skills, gained from his years working on news production for BBC TV, ITV and Sky News. This has involved him ploughing through over 3,000 articles to select an interesting mix of everyday life and national crises, good and bad news and intentional and un-intentional humour.

Some articles have been edited or shortened for easier reading. However, the writer's tenor has not been changed or enhanced in any way.

Due to age, most of the original magazine pages are discoloured and the print has faded. It has taken hundreds of hours using O.C.R. software and retyping to produce good quality text. We hope you will agree that it was all worth while.

Rosemary Jewers

(Patron of St. Andrew's Church, Lt. Massingham.)

PLEASE NOTE - The spelling, grammar and punctuation has been reproduced as originally printed. Some of the obvious printer's errors have been corrected.

Finally, all profit from the sale of this book will be shared between the existing participating Parochial Church Councils as agreed with them.

EVENTS OF INTEREST IN THE EARLY 1900s

1901   Edward VII became King.

1903   1st powered flight in the world by the Wright Bros. in the USA.

1903   Emmeline Pankhurst helped to form the Women's Social and Political Union to fight for votes for women.

1906   Eastern Counties Agricultural Labourers Union founded.

1907   Boy Scouts movement founded.

1908   Olympic games staged in London.

1908   National Farmers Union was founded.

1909   Old age pension payments began on 1st January.

1909   Louis Blériot made the first flight across the channel.

1909   F. W. Woolworth opened its first UK store.

1910   Edward VII died. George V became King.

1910   Dr Crippin arrested at sea for the murder of his wife.

1910   Florence Nightingale died.

1910   Girl Guide movement founded.

1914   First World War broke out.

1917   King Geoge V adopted Windsor surname.

1918   The Representation of the People Act gave the vote to every women aged 30 provided that she or her husband had property over a certain value.

1918   First World War ended.

1920   Dame Nellie Melba made first live radio entertainment broadcast on Marconi radio from Writtle, Chelmsford.

1921   The football association banned all women from playing on football league grounds.

1922   Daily BBC radio broadcasts began on 14th November.

1926   General strike.

1928   Woman were given equal voting rights with men. Every woman over the age of 21 could now vote in elections.

1928   Sir Alexander Fleming discovers Penicillin.

1930   Amy Johnson flew solo from Britain to Australia.

1932   Owing to widespread male unemployment the National Unemployed Workers' Movement organised the first of several hunger marches.

1933   Adolph Hitler became Chancellor of Germany.

MONEY & WEIGHT GUIDE

15th February 1971. A new decimal Currency was launched in the UK. The old pound note, shilling and penny coins were phased out over 18 months.

As money is mentioned in some articles a comparison from pounds, shillings and pennies (d) to today's currency may be useful.

The old currency was written as £2 : 5s : 4d. or £2/5/4
If just shillings and pennies as 5/4. If exactly 5 shillings as 5/-
If just pennies as 4d. If 4 and a half pence as 4½d.

12 pennies made 1 shilling. 20 shillings made £1
So there were 240 pennies in a £1
1 old penny (1d.) was worth less than half of the new pence (0.4166p)
1 old six pence (6d.) was worth 2.5 new pence
1 shilling (12d.) was worth 5 new pence
5 shillings (5/-) was worth 25 new pence
10 shillings (10/-) was worth 50 new pence (half of £1)
15 shillings (15/-) was worth 75 new pence
20 shillings or £1 was worth our £1

Other currencies: 1 Sovereign = £1   1 Guinea = £1 : 1 shilling

----

WEIGHT. 16 ounces made 1 pound, written as 1 lb. 1 pound in weight was just under half a kilo. 14 lbs made 1 stone.

The bushel was an old volume measure that was used for both liquid and dry goods. 1 bushel was equal to the volume of 8 Imperial gallons of liquid or the same amount of space that the liquid would take up, that any dry goods would fill. Put another way, in 1 cubic metre there would be nearly 27.5 bushels.

X

— THE —

PARISH MAGAZINE

FOR

ASHWICKEN,

CASTLE RISING, ROYDON,

GAYTON THORPE, EAST WALTON,

GRIMSTON, HILLINGTON,

LITTLE MASSINGHAM,

NORTH AND SOUTH WOOTTON,

WOLFERTON.

JANUARY, 1908.

King's Lynn:
PRINTED AND PUBLISHED BY W. H. TAYLOR, HIGH STREET.

This is the first cover of the new joint magazine. Over the years more parishes joined the group - CONGHAM, FLITCHAM, NORTH RUNCTON, SETCH AND HARDWICK, WEST WINCH, BABINGLEY, ANMER, WESTACRE.

Anmer and Westacre did not appear in later editions.

Extracts are included from the North Cranwich Deanery magazines during the 1912-1918 period.

XI

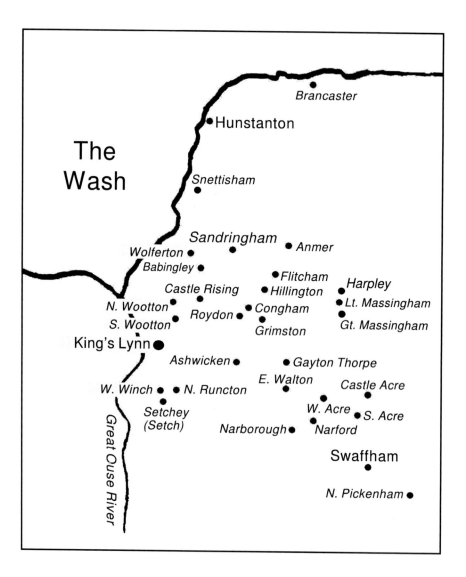

PARISH MAGAZINE.
1908

NORTH WOOTTON

THE COAL CLUB. - The Rector is intending to start a Coal Club for the parish on the first Monday in February. All those who wish to join should come to the Rectory between 10 and 12 in the morning of that day.

Members can subscribe to the Club each month from February to November, any sum they like. In November a bonus of 4/- will be added to every sovereign paid into the Club by that time. Mr. C. A. Howard has very generously promised a donation towards the Club which will probably pay for most if not all of the bonus.

It is hoped that many people in the parish will join the Club as a means of providing themselves with coal for next winter.

The price and quality of the coal will be settled by the subscribers.

SOUTH WOOTTON.

Owing to an outbreak of whooping-cough, the children's annual New Year party has been postponed; but the Choir and members of the Girls Friendly Society were entertained at the Rectory on the 16th, and dancing and various games made the evening pass all too quickly.

GAYTON THORPE & EAST WALTON

We welcome back Edward Alcock after his long stay in the Isle of Wight Sanatorium. He returns LOOKING the picture of health, but appearances are often deceitful. We must not anticipate the Doctor's Diagnosis.

LITTLE MASSINGHAM

Mrs. Birkbeck began the year by kindly inviting the School children to tea in the Parish room, and introducing a Ventriloquist and Conjuror to entertain them.

On Jan. 16th the Parish room proved too small to receive all who wished to be present at an excellent concert organized by Mr. Dring and Mr. Knights, for the purpose of starting a miniature Rifle Club. The net proceeds, amounting to nearly £7, will be practically sufficient to meet the preliminary expenses; whilst the subscriptions of the members (who must belong to the Parish, or to the Massingham Cricket Club, and be over the age of 14) and the sale of ammunition, should then keep the club self supporting.

ROYDON

The Rector regrets that he is unable to conduct the "Three Hours" Service this year, but advises those who appreciate the great privilege of attending that service to go to North Wootton, where it is being held for the first time.

GRIMSTON

The last enemy "Death" has been busy in our Parish of late. Five funerals in little over a fortnight. And then note the ages of the departed, ranging from 77 years to 3 days. Every stage of life is represented. What a lesson to us that this is not our home, but that "we seek one to come." We offer our sincerest sympathy to the many mourners.

CASTLE RISING & ROYDON

Suggestions for Lent

" If any man will come after, me, let him deny himself"

ALMSGIVING. Give more of your money, time or help, to those who have greater need.

PRAYER. Come to Holy Communion regularly. Read the Bible daily. Make a special self-examination and confess your sins. Come to church on week-days as often as you can.

FASTING. Give up something you are fond of, such as beer, sugar, smoking, etc.

ASHWICKEN

Bible Society Meeting. On Thursday, Feb. 6th, a meeting was held in the schoolroom in aid of the funds of the British and Foreign Bible Society. The room was nearly full.

After a few words of introduction by the Rector, in which he endeavoured to impress upon all those present the immense importance of the work done by the Society, emphasising especially the fact that all the great Missionary Societies of the world would practically be paralysed without its help in translating the Scriptures into more than 400 different languages. A most interesting address was given by the Rev. H. Starmer, who spoke principally about the work done in Korea, and gave a description of how the extreme and well nigh hopeless difficulty of gaining an entrance into that country was overcome in a most Providential way.

Their initial hindrances were both numerous and great, as no foreigner was allowed to enter the country, and the colporteur could find no one willing to teach him the language. However, the door was at last opened in a manner which plainly showed the finger of God. The ship of a rich merchant was wrecked in a storm, and all the valuable cargo lost. The owner, reduced to poverty, was in his distress prevailed upon for a certain sum to teach the Korean language to the Bible man, and so at last a translation of the Holy Scriptures entered the country. The collection after was £1/2/6.

NORTH WOOTTON

BURIAL.

March 23rd, Caroline Pigg, aged 65.

May she rest in peace.

She was a great sufferer, yet most patient. She died in faith, and we earnestly hope full of repentance.

PARISH MAGAZINE.
1908

CASTLE RISING & ROYDON

By the sudden demise of James Barwood, a familiar figure has been removed from our midst. He was an honest hard working old man. Out in all weathers, nothing seemed to deter him from his purpose. It was probably his over anxiety to get to work too soon after a sharp attack of Bronchitis, that hastened his dissolution. He died in harness, may he rest in peace. A vacancy is thus created in the Earl of Northampton's Charity of £26 a year. Applicants may be either married or single, and of either sex, must have been bona fide residents in the Parish of Castle Rising for not less than four years previous to their appointment, and must be unable to maintain themselves by their own exertions by reason of age, ill health, accident or infirmity.

The death of General Sir Redvers Buller came as a shock to the people at Castle Rising. It was known that he had been seriously indisposed for some time, but that his end was so near was quite unexpected. He passed away at Downes, Crediton, on Tuesday, June 2nd, in his 70th year. His loss will be greatly felt at Castle Rising, where he has managed the Estate for a number of years. Of his public career it is not for us to speak here; the London and local papers have given a full and detailed description. The affection and respect in which he was held by all classes was borne ample witness to at the military funeral which the Authorities accorded to him. Nothing less would have satisfied the public sentiment. Such a scene of solemn splendour is rarely produced. It was the spontaneous tribute of a nation's affection to one of the bravest and best of her sons. The King and the Prince of Wales were represented at the funeral, as well as the Army and Navy. And the whole County of Devon were mourning the loss of their hero. Hundreds of wreaths, with expressions of sympathy, came from all quarters, amongst them a beautiful one from the tenantry on the Castle Rising Estate.

The coffin bore this inscription-

"Redvers Henry Buller, of Downes, General. Colonel Commandant of the King's Royal Rifle Corps, V.C., G.C.B., G.C.M.G., P.C. Born Dec. 7th, 1839, died 2nd June, 1908."

It must have been a sight never to be forgotten by those who saw it, when the coffin was lowered into the grave and the "Last Post" was sounded by twenty buglers of the King's Royal Rifles.

GRIMSTON

U.M.C.A. - The Coral League have made strong scouring cloths, to be sold for the benefit of the Mission. Please send orders to Miss D. Thursby, price 6d.

PARISH MAGAZINE.
1908

GAYTON THORPE & EAST WALTON

THE CRICKET CLUB has met with varying fortune since last its doings were here recorded. Further particulars are postponed, as the scoring books are not at present available for reference, the scorer having taken them to Snettisham. Whether this be in the hope that sea breezes will somehow impart greater vigour to their future records, who can say?

THE DAY SCHOOLS have lately been closed for more than a week by order of the M.O.H., owing to an outbreak of scarlet fever. Only one household has been attacked, up to the present, and now the trouble appears to be fast dying out. The reprehensible conduct of a young West-Acre woman, who had been procured by the Vicar as a help to the overtaxed mother of *eight* invalids, was calculated to spread the epidemic far afield. We presume that the M.O.H. has taken steps to punish this wilful and wicked breach of the law. Much sympathy should go out, and we hope has gone out, to the father and the plucky mother of these little patients. Thanks to their splendid constitutions, the whole family are now rapidly recovering health and spirits.

Most unfortunately the epidemic has done mischief in another direction. The Burtons were within sight of extra rewards for unbroken attendance, but they have been forbidden to attend the Schools. Thus, away go all hopes of obtaining silver watches from the County Committee. A little bird has however sung so encouraging a song into our ear, that we strongly advise these indefatigable Schoolgoers to maintain their excellent record, so soon as they are permitted to return to their lessons.

This is the second occasion (vide the June magazine) on which we have had cause to mention the Regulations laid down by the County Committee concerning attendance. We hope the combined wisdom of that august Body of Educational Adepts will find some way of altering a Rule, which they cannot but recognise as most discouraging.

GRIMSTON

OURS is indeed a heavy death roll this month. Made up it will be seen chiefly with the names of quite young children; all of whom, with one exception, fell victims to the measles and whooping cough epidemic in Pott Row.

One cannot but think that so many losses from these common and well known diseases are greater than they should have been. Were proper precautions taken to avoid the diseases spreading? Was the necessary and proper care taken in all cases? God forbid that it should be hinted that there has

PARISH MAGAZINE.
1908

been anything approaching wilful neglect. Still in matters of life and death even ignorance is blameable.

Many think it would have been wiser to have closed the School at an early period. And then again, was the fact sufficiently realized that even in the simplest cases of measles, too great care cannot possibly be taken in keeping patients warm and sheltered, and guarding them against the slightest risk of chill or cold.

In view of what has happened in Pott Row, we must earnestly trust that very special precautions and care will be taken now that these complaints have appeared, as was only to be expected, in the 'Grimston Town' part of the Parish.

It should be mentioned that the School Managers at a meeting on June 22nd, sent a very urgent recommendation, which is all they could do, to the Sanitary Authority, that the Church Hill School should be closed for a time at least.

Photos of Pott Row on page 32

IT is proposed to take our Sunday School children for a day at Hunstanton as their treat this year. This must partly depend upon the kindness of those who have waggons to lend to convey them. The Rector would be grateful for contributions to help towards the increased expenses of this form of Treat. One contribution of 5/- has already been very kindly promised.

WOLFERTON

A VERY interesting Ladies' Cricket match took place at Wolferton on June 20th, against Gentlemen, who played left handed with broom-sticks, which resulted in a win for the Gentlemen by about 30 runs. Both teams were kindly entertained to tea by the Rev. F. A. S. ffolkes, in the Rectory grounds, and his kindness was much appreciated. The match afforded great amusement to a large number of Parishioners.

LITTLE MASSINGHAM

We have again to chronicle some exceptional weather. The third week of July proved one of the wettest weeks in hay time people recall in this Parish. Unfortunately several acres of hay had not been carted and some were not even on cock. But it is probably safe to say that the other crops, both corn and root, have more than made up in value the considerable loss on the hay.

THINGS OLD. "In the history of Norwich it is recorded among the remarkable events, that in 1745 fine flour, from Hertfordshire, was retailed in Norwich, before which time a coarse household bread, inferior to meal, was the general bread used in the city and county. Barley bread was till that time as common as it is now in some parts of Wales. Till that period, scarcely any wheat was

5

grown in this part of the country. Within the last thirty years not more than 30 or 40 acres of wheat were grown in Little Massingham, and now there are between 300 and 400 acres. The growth of this corn favourably affects the condition of the peasantry, by supplying a large quantity of gleaning as well as work. The thirty families belonging to this parish have the gleaning of three or four hundred acres of wheat, and many of the families collect from 8 to 12 and even 16 bushels. The earnings of the women and children by this means have often amounted to more than the earnings of the labourer himself in harvest." 1825.

GAYTON THORPE & EAST WALTON

(Did this man really die twice? Ed.)

Here again death has taken away GEORGE HERRING JUDE, for so he was christened 68 years ago, at a time when English mothers took great care never to leave their little ones long without the unseen, though none the less real, embrace of The Saviour's Arms, by means of the Sacrament of Holy Baptism. He was buried on July 18th, and it was most gratifying to see at the grave side the young master paying a last tribute of regard to the memory of the old labourer.

ROYDON

The offertory for the Pan-Anglican Thank was £1.

GRIMSTON

AUGUST has been the month of our Summer Treats and Outings. First on Friday, Aug. 7th, came the Sunday School Treat. This consisted of a day in Hunstanton. Waggons to convey nearly 100 children and teachers, were most kindly provided by Messrs. R. Coe, Saunders and Spragg. Each child received a bag containing sandwiches and buns for lunch, and the whole party, consisting of exactly 100, had tea together at Roy's Restaurant and Dining Rooms. The day was beautifully fine, and a very enjoyable day was spent. Our best thanks are due to those who lent the waggons. The Rector begs to thank very cordially the following for their kind contributions: - Mr. J. Dix 5/-, Mr. R. Ashley 5/-, Mrs. Rippingill 5/-.

A great want just now in the Mission room is new chairs. The old chairs, which have lasted 23 years, are rapidly breaking up through 'dry rot', and we shall soon be reduced to none. Two contributions, 10/- and 5/-, have already been received through Mr. Wheeler. Further gifts are urgently invited.

HILLINGTON

THE Wedding on August 10th of Robert Howell and Elizabeth Martha Hammond, excited more than ordinary interest, owing to Miss Hammond's having been for many years assistant teacher in the School. There was a large assemblage of spectators, who unanimously pronounced it to be one of the prettiest weddings they had ever witnessed.

LITTLE MASSINGHAM

THE County Council are holding a course of 10 butter-making Lectures in the Parish Room. It was felt that a distinct improvement in the local butter followed similar lectures held fifteen years ago, and it is hoped that many will avail themselves of this year's course.

THINGS OLD. - Extract from Massingham Parva. – "In 1824 the villages of Norfolk were not the quiet orderly places they are now. In Great Massingham in that year there were cases of burglary, issuing of base coin, sheep, pig, corn and fowl stealing, besides poaching and other offences. The house of one of the labourers was searched, and in it were found base coin, silver and gold, corn and other articles, the apparatus for house-breaking - vice, files, dark lantern, and fifty picklock keys, which would open almost all the doors in both parishes. It was customary for most of the labourers to spend their nights gaming at this house. During the same time three persons were transported away from Great Massingham, and many others imprisoned".

THINGS OLD. - A family connected with Little Massingham was that of the Le Stranges of Hunstanton. They held lands in Congham and Little Massingham from a very early date. John Le Strange, who died in 1517, left directions in his will that if he died within five miles of Little Massingham, he should be buried in the church, in the chapel of our Lady; and that in any case a tomb should be erected in that chapel to his memory. This was done by William Mordaunt. The stone tomb, bereft of all its brasses, and removed from its Original position, now stands in the tower. Until quite recently it was customary for the parish clerk, when chiming the three bells, to grasp one rope with each hand, and to place his foot in a loop in the third rope, while he stood with his other leg upon the convenient platform which the old Le Strange tomb afforded him.

GRIMSTON

IT was a great source of regret to all of us that our flag could not be hoisted on Nov. 9th, when the King passed through the village, but though every effort was made, it was found impossible from the rotten state of the wire cord. It would have been fitting too to have greeted His Majesty with a peal on the bells. The bells were, however, rung in the King's honour in the evening.

Workers on Thompson's farm, North Wootton in 1899 *(Mary Cook)*
Left to right ...? Robert Merrikin, S. Raines, A. Graver, ...? N. Twite,
T. Potter, Fred Merrikin, Edward Merrikin, H. Hardy, J. Woodfield.

(T. Jewers)

An example of a steam engine used in the early 1900s, as a power source for threshing corn (or thrashing as it was called in Norfolk). One like this, is almost certainly to have been used to power the elevator in the top picture. Steam engines were still used by some farmers until the combine harvester became affordable. CLAAS developed the first self-propelled combine harvester in 1953.

Sunday outing to Narborough Aerodrome 1916. *Sketch by Timothy O'Brien*
(Narborough Research Group)

In the early 1900s, trains were an option, but horse-drawn vehicles were still used for mass transportation of people by road, as shown in the drawing above.

However, group outings for a day trip to the seaside from villages as described by parsons in their magazines, would probably have meant the passengers travelling in horse drawn wagons or carts loaned by local farmers. These wagons would normally have been used on the farms for moving grain, root crops, animal foods etc.

(T. Jewers)
Sketches of the Wright Bros. plane

In 1903 the Wright Brothers made the first powered flight in the world.

Having discovered how to keep a plane airborne, many others wanted to do better. In 1909 Louis Blériot became the first man to fly across the Channel. Soon larger planes were being built and it is recorded that the first commercial flight took place on 1st January 1914. The route was between St. Petersburg and Tampa, Florida.

(T. Jewers)

Although in its infancy in the early 1900s, a more luxurious mode of transportation - the motor car - was being developed for those who could afford it. The picture above shows a Peugeot car made in 1904,

(T. Jewers)

An estate version of the model T built in 1924

However, it was not very long before the possibility of a cheap car became a reality, when Henry Ford in America, announced that he wanted to build an affordable car for the mass market. The product which made his name and fortune was his model - T.

Between 1908-1928 15,000,000 of these were manufactured.

Henry Ford was reputed to have said that the car could be supplied in any colour as long as it was black. Whether this was true or not - the legend lives on. The model T was widely know as the "Tin Lizzy".

After the first World War, Ford established production plants in several countries, including a factory at Dagenham, Essex.

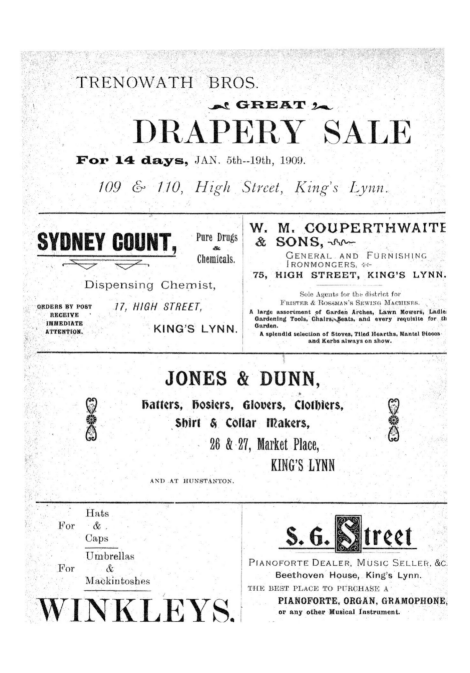

11

ANMER

During Advent there was a successful work party once a week, making garments for the Church of England Waifs and Strays. The material and tea were provided chiefly through the kindness of Mrs. Hamilton and Mrs. Stanton, and there was an average attendance of fourteen, who made some excellent garments, which ought to be much appreciated this cold weather.

The attendance at the daily services reached a total of over a thousand by Christmas Day, that is, since they were started at the end of July last. The side chapel is not overcrowded even now, and there would be no difficulty in finding a seat for anyone who would like to come in the future!

FLITCHAM

Among the chief events during the past month was the tea given by the Queen to the children in the Day School on Her Majesty's Birthday. It was followed by a capital programme of songs, recitations, &c.

NORTH WOOTTON

THE COAL CLUB. - The coal club has closed its year very successfully. Just over 18 tons of coal was purchased with money paid in by the members. The coal is giving good satisfaction.

GAYTON THORPE & EAST WALTON

LENDING LIBRARY. - Mrs. Beauchamp requests that all books be returned to her at once, as she is leaving for China shortly. We wish her God-speed and a happy meeting with Mr. Beauchamp, who is working so zealously as an English Priest among the Chinese, to whose spiritual welfare he has devoted so large a part of his life.

THE MOTHERS UNION had a successful gathering in the school on Dec. 16th, when many members foregathered, in neighbourly love and concord, and were earnestly addressed by Miss Barclay, and whose helpful words we are most grateful for.

CASTLE RISING & ROYDON

U.M.C.A. CORAL LEAGUE. - The junior members of the above met as usual on S. Andrew's Day, to open the mission boxes. As a result of the year's collecting and the sale of scouring cloths, £2/15/9 was sent to Miss Herring for our African boy. She writes: "Please thank all who have helped to send this very much indeed. Let the boys join too to help the African child whom you at Castle Rising are bringing up as a Christian child should be brought up. Thank the children for writing to Yustus Kumalemba."

PARISH MAGAZINE.
1909

ASHWICKEN

CAROL SINGING. - On the evenings of Dec. 30th and 31st, a band of Carol singers consisting of Miss Rolfe, Mr. Starnes, Miss Constance and Miss Naomi Groom, accompanied by the children of our choir, paraded our village. The sum of 12/8 was collected for Waifs and Strays.

NORTH WOOTTON

THE Parish Magazine for last year was so far successful financially, that at the end of the year I was in pocket to the extent of 2/6, which I have put to the Sick and Poor Fund, a fund which is kept going by the collections at Holy Communion. But had it not been for the money received by the Editor for advertisements, things might not have been in so satisfactory a state.

LITTLE MASSINGHAM

The Rifle Shooting has shewn signs of reviving. A special "Christmas Dinner" competition brought several members to try for half-a-dozen prizes. Unfortunately the goose went to Great Massingham.

THE children of the parish had a delightful treat given by Mrs. Birkbeck on Jan. 14th. They were invited to tea in the parish room, where a Christmas tree loaded with presents, sweets and crackers, had been prepared. Each child received besides a parcel of clothing. The parishioners wish to thank Mrs. Birkbeck for her great kindness.

CASTLE RISING & ROYDON

ROYDON. - THE new school building grows apace, but the subscription list does not mount up quite so satisfactorily. Since our last issue a donation of £1/1/0 by Mr. Edward Pratt has to be acknowledged, and one of £5 by Mrs. W. Thursby, and Mr. Everard besides giving £25, has guaranteed £5 a year towards the re-payment of the loan of £100. This was not mentioned last month. It is proposed to hold a Jumble Sale in aid of the fund after harvest.

MEDICAL CLUB. - It is possible that some of our readers may not know of the existence of the Medical Club, and for their benefit the rules are printed below. Owing to an annual subscription given by Capt. C. A. Howard, the fees are exceedingly low, and the best medical attendance is afforded practically free of cost. The membership at the present time is lower than it has been for 40 years. Two reasons may account for this, either that the people of Castle Rising are wonderfully well off, or that they are unaware of the existence of the Club.

Details are listed below:

PARISH MAGAZINE.
1909

CLOTHING CLUB. - There is also a Clothing Club which gives a bonus of 3/- in the £ at the end of the year, when this is compared with the rate of interest given by the P.O. Savings Bank, which is 6d in the £, it is unaccountable that not more than six people avail themselves of this encouraging aid to thrift. The payments for this are taken at the same time as those to the Medical Club, viz.: 1st Monday in each month from 9 to 10 a.m. at the Rectory.

MEDICAL CLUB RULES.

1.- MEMBERSHIP. Persons must be in good health on joining the Club.
2. Members may be admitted at any time, payments commencing from the beginning of the quarter during which they are admitted.
3. Honorary Members can nominate one adult for every 10/- annual subscription.
4.- PAYMENTS. Married couples, 9/- a year. Single adults, 6/- a year. Children under 16 years, 8d a year. Confinements, £1/1/0.
5. Payments to be made in advance on the 1st Monday in each month at the Rectory, between 9 and 10 in the morning - members to bring their cards and to see that their payments are properly marked.
6. - MEDICAL ATTENDANCE. The Doctor will see members daily at the Surgery, Grimston, from 9 to 10 a.m., and from 7 to 8 p.m.
7. Members needing the Doctor's attendance at other times to apply to the Rector for a note.
8. Members are required to provide their own bottles.

CASTLE RISING, NORTH WOOTTON AND ROYDON NURSING ASSOCIATION.

Application for the Nurse to be made to Mrs Thursby.

Payments to be made as follows :

ANNUAL SUBSCRIPTIONS.

Class 1, Labourers, 2/-. Class 2, Gentlemen's servants, carpenters, school teachers, etc., 3/- Class 3, Farmers and others, 5/- to 10/-.

FEES

Class.	Per week with board and lodging.	Visits	12 hours and board.
1	2/-	Free	4d
2	3/-		6d
3	5/- to 10/-		9d to 1/6

FEES FOR NON-SUBSCRIBERS
For visits from Nurse, 4d; to Nurse 2d.

For CONFINEMENTS for Subscribers, Class 1, 5/- Notice of not less than three months must be given, otherwise fees are double. For non-residents and non-subscribers the fees are double.

When the house is one of Classes 1 and 2, the Nurse will be required to do as much as she reasonably can of the household work, except the family washing.

WANTS. - Will someone please take pity on the bare walls of Nurse's rooms, and give her a few pictures?

Orders wanted by the G.F.S. and Coral workers for scouring cloths, and little children's petticoats and overalls.

CASTLE RISING & ROYDON

THE Rector has been advised to take a sea voyage in order to help him to recover from the effects of his recent attack of influenza. Consequently he started on Wednesday the 24th on H.M.S. Swiftsure for a cruise in the Mediterranean. He hopes to be home on Easter Day.

FLITCHAM

THE good news of His Majesty's gracious intention to present an organ to our church, was not public when the *Parish Magazine* for March went to press, and was therefore omitted. Since then it has become generally known, and our readers will have seen notice of it in their newspapers. However, we wish to record it here, as an expression of deep and lasting gratitude to His Majesty. It is our earnest hope that the new organ will be to the greater glory of Almighty God, in adding beauty to our church, dignity to our worship, and *numbers to our congregation.* We hope that the organ will be in its place by Easter Day.

GAYTON THORPE & EAST WALTON

THE MOTHERS UNION foregathered on March 12th, when the vicar addressed 17 members on Woman's Home Work. He selected the story of a London lad who told his Bishop what his father and he earned to keep the family going, what work they did and how mother lighted the fire in the morning to get their breakfasts ready, then looked after "the kids" and sent them to School, how she tidied up and got ready dinner and supper, and so forth. The Bishop enquired what wages this lad and his father earned, and what the mother earned also toward the up-keeping of the house. To which the lad replied - "Father gets so much, and I get so much, but mother gets no wages at all because she does no work." The moral is this. The best work a woman can do is HOME WORK, although perhaps it makes no show in the world outside. After all it's Woman's Home influence that tells. The Suffragists may have something to say for themselves, it is a poor cause indeed that has nothing. The tendency, however, of the Suffragists' agitation is to make women discontented with home influences, and with woman's work pure and simple, and to lead them to intrude upon the work which God intended for man to do, as quite apart from the work of his co-partner. Do not let the woman go beyond her apron strings.

WESTACRE

The High House Reading Room paid Westacre Reading Room a visit on Tuesday night, 16th March, to compete at games. The result was in favour of Westacre both in dominoes and bagatelle.

1909

LITTLE MASSINGHAM

THE Rev. H. H. Ashley Nash again brought his cinematograph, on March 18th, to illustrate the work the Society for Promoting Christianity amongst the Jews is undertaking. Our contributions were specially asked for in aid of the hospital for poor sick Jews at Jerusalem.

WE have been reading with interest and some anxiety in the daily papers the account of the collision of an iceberg with the ship in which Mrs. Knights and her large family sailed for Canada. The passengers seem all to have been safely landed at St. John's, and been transferred to a fresh ship to take them on to Montreal. We are awaiting fuller news of the mishap, which we hope to receive soon from Mrs. Knights, and meanwhile, we trust that, if they were alarmed, they have suffered no real misfortune from the accident, beyond delay and the change of vessels.

Photos on page 33 - 34

GAYTON THORPE & EAST WALTON

MISSIONARY BOXES. - When visiting some sick for the Rector of Ashwicken, I was recently waylaid by - shall I say "a tramp," or a "foot-pad," or an enthusiastic lady? - Who presented, not a pistol to my head, but a missionary box to my gaze, as though to say, "Money and no excuse." I learnt that, that very box had been opened for 7 successive years and collected over £9 in that time. This made me ask myself why we should not do ditto. This year therefore I propose to distribute a few boxes, to be opened on or about July 1st and Dec. 31st. Who will take a box?

GAYTON THORPE. - The question of the Parish boundaries has been lately revived. The Brick Kiln houses are in Thorpe and not in Gayton. And what is more, they are also in the East Walton Educational area, although, as it happens at the present time, children from the Brick Kilns attend Gayton School. This is owing to their having previously gone to that School. The Gayton School Authorities have the power to refuse, and undoubtedly would in most cases refuse, admittance to our Thorpe children. It is hardly fair for the Gayton Managers to pick and choose from children outside their own area, accepting those they see well to accept, and refusing all others. We repeat, this is hardly fair to East Walton, and is very unsportsman like.

WESTACRE

THE hand of death has been very heavy on Westacre just lately. Mr. William Hunter, at an early age, has received his call. He was brought by his own wish back to Westacre, where he had spent most of his life.

1909

FLITCHAM

NOTE. - The Vicar will be glad to know, *within a week,* if any subscriber fails to obtain the current number of the magazine.

THE Services in Holy Week were well attended on Wednesday and Thursday. On the other days they had to be postponed in order to give the organ builders time to finish the erection of His Majesty's gracious gift.

GAYTON THORPE & EAST WALTON

MOTOR AND BICYCLE ACCIDENT. - We congratulate, whilst we condole with Charles Causton, of Thorpe, on his providential escape from what might have been a very much more serious accident. We can sympathise with him over his accident, because bicycle mis-adventures have come our way and broken our bones as many times as we have fingers on one hand. To be thrown to hard mother earth is bad enough, but to have a motor car on the top - ugh! no, thank you.

WESTACRE

THE church clock is now complete and keeping good time - so far there has only been one irregularity, and that was in the striking. However, it was no fault of the clock, but for some unknown reason the wires that were holding the big weight had become twisted.

Besides telling us the correct time, the clock is also a great improvement to the look of the tower, and go where we will, we shall not see a more handsome clock than ours with its appropriate text, " WATCH AND PRAY," in place of figures 1 - 12.

Photo on page 34

NORTH WOOTTON.

GIFT TO THE CHURCH. - On Whitsunday was used for the first time the new bread box, which has been given to the church by five communicants. It is round in shape, of solid silver, and gilt inside. All that has to do with the altar must be of the very best; and owing to the loving care which has in the past been expended upon our sanctuary, we are better off in this respect than many churches. Several improvements however could be made, even now the most needful of which is the raising of the altar upon another step or steps. If this could be carried out, our worship would be much helped.

FLITCHAM

CHURCHYARD. – It is with regret we have to record that so few responded to the Vicar's appeal to work in the churchyard. For it is surprising that those who frequent their parish church should allow the last resting place of their relatives and friends to remain in such a disgraceful condition. The Vicar is strongly of the opinion that this work should be a labour of love; for who could wish to see this turned into a matter of pounds, shillings and pence? Is it too much to hope that, on his return, the Vicar will find God's acre more what it should be?

ANMER

IT is now possible to see how beautiful a building the new Reading Room will be, which His Majesty The King so generously is having built for Anmer. It is already a great addition to the picturesqueness of the place.

As apparently there are so many wild rumours flying about, it may be a good thing to say here that the Rector is proposing to take a three weeks holiday on August 14th. Through the generosity of an old friend it will take the form of a trip to visit Christiania, Stockholm, Copenhagen, Saint Petersburg, and possibly Moscow, and one or two other places on the shores of the Baltic. He will be home again (D.V.) to take duty on the first Sunday in September. During his absence Mr Stephens Vicar of Flitcham will stand in.

HILLINGTON

ON the 6th of July the Union Jack on the school lawn was flying in honour of Princess Victoria's birthday. It was also the 16th anniversary of the wedding of T.R.H. The Prince and Princess of Wales.

Harvest began generally about 18th August in this district under not very favourable conditions.

NORTH WOOTTON.

A HEARTY welcome to Mr. and Mrs. Coulton, who have come to live amongst us. We pray that the Divine Blessing may rest upon them in their life here. May they find in our church what so many of us are learning to find there, viz., the strength and comfort of our Blessed Lord's ever abiding Presence. May they benefit too from our bright, pure, health-giving air.

THE COMING HARVEST. Harvest is once more drawing near; and the Divine Promise that "while the earth remaineth, seed time and harvest shall not cease," is again about to have its fulfilment. May we learn many and new lessons from the harvest this year, best of all, the spirit of true thankfulness towards Him "in Whom we live and move, and have our being." And there is something more to be said.

Harvest time is always a time of danger for the men at work in the fields, the work is hard, the hours long, and the sun very hot, the temptation to take too much beer is difficult to resist. God of His mercy help us all this harvest to

1909

keep our bodies in temperance. Let wives and mothers do what they can to help husbands and sons in this matter.

GAYTON THORPE & EAST WALTON

BACK from "our" holiday! Dropping the third person, I will write in the first. But perhaps I should apologise for writing at all, for outside my own inner circle who cares whither I went and what I did! Well! I'll risk it...

THE annual outing of our Church workers and Sunday School children took place on Saturday, Aug. 14th. Between fifty and sixty started in two parties, the one from Thorpe, for East Winch station, in a waggon lent by Mr. Youngman, the other from Walton, for Narborough, conveyed there by Mr. Knight. Meeting and mingling in Lynn, the "united party" sped on to Hunstanton, where a pleasant day was passed.

In these all too careless days, when both the "simple" Word of God and "sound doctrine" are alike becoming less and less valued, it is a matter of congratulation that we are lucky to have a Mistress who so well instructs the children in "the fear of God," which is "the beginning of wisdom," and as *persona in parochiâ* I rejoice that the parents are wise enough, and generous minded and trustful enough to trust the weekly religious training of the little ones to such good hands.

ANMER

ON Saturday, August 17th, the choir, favoured by fine weather, had an enjoyable afternoon on Snettisham beach. The tide was too far out to enable everyone actually to reach the sea, but a good deal of enjoyment was obtained by 'cockling' in the wet sand.

HILLINGTON

ON Coronation Day, August 9th, the Union Jack was hoisted from the flag-staff in the school grounds, and the children sang "God save the King." The School broke up on the 13th August for five weeks' holiday.

ROYDON

ON Thursday, Sept. 9th, the Roydon School children were most hospitably entertained by Mr. and the Misses Everard at the Lodge. After tea their kind hosts were most resourceful in providing amusements and quite a novelty among these were the launching of two Zeppelin Air-ships, which accomplished record flights, being last sighted over Congham church tower.

FLITCHAM

CHURCHYARD. - The Vicar begs to return grateful thanks to those who have kindly cut the grass in the churchyard during his absence from home. After harvest, we hope some volunteers will be found ready to come and put in a little work in order to make God's Acre as tidy as possible for the winter months.

ASHWICKEN

ASSOCIATION FOR REWARDING SKILLED LABOUR.

The annual meeting was held at Hillington on Wednesday, Sept. 29th, and our parish may well feel proud of its record. Of our seven competitors only one failed to obtain a prize, and he would have been successful in obtaining a third had the Class in which he was entered been more fully represented. The following is a list of prize-winners:

Champion Hedging prize,
1st Ben Daws.

Traction Engine Knowledge,
1st W. Starling.

Reaper Knowledge,
or Self Binder,
1st W. Mason, 2nd J. Clark.

Lads' Ploughing,
3rd Thomas Reeve.

Driving Competition,
2nd Thomas Reeve.

Best Shepherd's Dog,
1st E. Smith, (Jack).

Best turn out of Plough horses,
2nd Thomas Reeve.

NORTH WOOTTON

I beg of you - at least those of you who have been Confirmed - to begin on All Saints' Day to keep some such rule as this: -
(1) Pray at home every morning and night.
(2) Read every day a few verses from the Gospels.
(3) Let NOTHING WHATEVER keep you away from Church. Go EVERY Lord's Day.
(4) Make an earnest and reverent Communion on the first *or* third Sunday in every month.

OUR good friend, Miss Eastwood, has written to me to ask you all again this year to buy your Christmas cards of her. The profit made by the sale of these cards is given to help the work of the Church of S. Peter, London Docks. Many of you know how hard it is to carry on Christian work in that desperately poor and very wicked part of London. You will, I am certain, out of affection and respect for Miss Eastwood, be ready to help her in supporting this good work. She will shortly be sending a selection of cards for you to choose from.

GRIMSTON

Miss Coe kindly brought down to the Rectory for a special treat, a party from S. Luke's of about 30 little ones in a dog cart. They were packed together like sardines in a tin. Most of the teachers were at the Rectory to entertain them.

PARISH MAGAZINE.
1909

ANMER

ON November 8th, Monday, Anmer had the great honour of a visit from Their Majesties The King and Queen to open the New Reading Room which His Majesty so kindly has had built for our village. Fortunately the weather was glorious, and a great gathering of Anmer folk assembled about 3 o'clock to greet Their Majesties: who arrived soon after half-past three, and proceeded to the Library, where the committee awaited them.

The King, after looking at a copy of the Rules presented to him, then went into the main room, and declared the building open. In a few kindly words he expressed his great interest in all that concerned the welfare of those who worked for him on the Sandringham estate, and hoped that the new reading room would be a place for recreation and enjoyment after the day's work. Three most hearty cheers was the response which came at once from all those gathered there.

ASHWICKEN

SCHOOL. - A meeting of Managers was called to consider the alterations in the school buildings demanded by the Board of Education. Unfortunately only two Managers were able to be present, and as it requires three to form a quorum, the meeting was postponed.

FLITCHAM

The following letter of grateful thanks has been received by the Vicar from the Matron: -

"West Norfolk and Lynn Hospital, King's Lynn. Oct. 8, '09.

Dear Sir, Will you convey to your parishioners my very grateful thanks (on behalf of the Patients) for the vegetables, fruit, eggs and butter which were sent from Flitcham Harvest Festival: also for the cheque for £3/5/0. The Patients thoroughly enjoyed the good things. Yours faithfully, (sgd) Helen Swain, Matron.

While we appreciate all the Matron's remarks, we ought not to rest satisfied with our efforts; but to try, next year, to give still more: and, as a mark of real gratitude to Almighty God, for His many blessings.

GAYTON THORPE & EAST WALTON

YET another incident. Those of our readers who kept last year's numbers of the *Parish Magazine* will find remarks "Connected with our Dead," (*vide* the February issue). The rector then expressed his appreciation of "the ritual of passing the coffin under the crossed staffs," and his readiness to have any hymn sung "to the living God." Now it so happens that, as on that occasion, so on a recent one, our worthy and highly esteemed parish clerk employed a friend to dig the grave,

PARISH MAGAZINE.
1909 -1910

because that grave was for one of the clerk's own relations; in the first instance for his son, and in the second for his brother. This stranger, who certainly dug a most tidy grave, desired to introduce certain prayers and hymns connected with "the Shepherds." The rector on the second occasion, in keeping with last year's notice, objected, but owing to the extreme persistency of the stranger's request, he yielded so far as to say he would read the address himself, and would also permit the hymn to be sung, if it were altered from "O Death" to "Almighty God." Thus a threatened unpleasantness (introduced by a stranger) was averted. It was most painful to the rector. Now, in the hymn, the following statement was found to be put into the lips of the mourners-

"And from the moral code of God
He never did depart."

We appeal to any and every reader to say whether such a statement could ever be truthfully said even of the *best of men?* This has only to be read to see how "wordy" it is, and how totally lacking in dignity or beauty of diction. It talks of "the corpse," and uses words almost as polysyllabic as "the blessed word Mesopotamia," or even as "Constantinopolitanus." Thus the rector asks to be relieved from any recurrence of these quite unnecessary, certainly unseemly, and undoubtedly to him at least, most painful incidents.

WOLFERTON

THE Boy Scouts, under the control of the Rector, are meeting twice a week at the school for the practice of boxing and single-stick, and all other matters of interest to scouts. The leader of the patrol is David Godfrey. Boy scouting, which has become so popular, was started by General Sir R. Baden-Powell, the famous defender of Mafeking, and if carried out in a proper manner, must be for the improvement of the boys.

1910

From the Editorial in the January magazine. Ed.

We are only able to keep the price of the magazine to each subscriber as low as one penny, by the help afforded us from the payments of the advertisers. These payments are of great importance to our budget, and were they to fall off, a heavy deficit would be the result and, alas, we have no Chancellor of the Exchequer at hand to devise new sources of revenue. Will, then, all the subscribers to the magazines, before their shopping excursions into Lynn, kindly run their eyes over the advertisements, and see if they cannot provide for their wants from some of the places of business mentioned there? This would be a help both to the Magazine and some return justly deserved to those who, no doubt, partly from business enterprise, but also from the desire to help our PARISH MAGAZINE, very kindly make use of it for advertising purposes.

ANMER

SINCE our last number was issued the children of Anmer School were entertained at tea on December 1st, by the kindness of H.M. The Queen, in commemoration of H.M.'s birthday: and a happy evening was spent with games and general fun.

CASTLE RISING & ROYDON

My dear Parishioners, - The country will shortly be involved in the throes of a General Election. The issues before the electorate are of paramount importance, as well as of very great difficulty. Therefore it behoves every man who has the right to vote, to consider very seriously his responsibility on this critical occasion. There is one thing that I feel sure of, and that is that Religion should stand before Party. In this free country every man has a right to his religious opinions, and a right to see that his children are brought up in his own faith. One political party denies this right. They say the State ought to decide what religion is taught in the Schools, and not the parent. This is religious intolerance, and in my judgement no candidate for Parliament should be supported unless he promises to uphold the right of parents to determine the character of all the religious instruction to be given to their children in the Schools.

The subjoined questions have been sent to both candidates for this division of Norfolk. Mr. Jodrell has promised to uphold this principle. Sir George White has sent no reply: but it is well known that he is committed to a policy by which the State and not the parent shall say what religion the child shall learn, and which would then forbid any definite religious teaching being given in any School. What is wanted is equal treatment for all - Church teaching for Church children - Nonconformist: for all the Nonconformist children - the Parents' faith for every child.

Therefore, I think that all

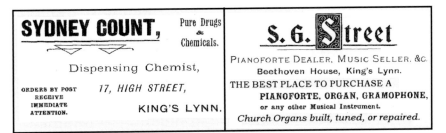

1910

Churchmen and others who are in favour of religious freedom, whatever political party they happen to admire on other grounds, should put religion first and record their votes for the man who is pledged to support these principles. We do not know what may be in store for us in the future, but we can all pray to God that the history we are going to make, may be to His Glory.

Old Castle Rising photo of the 5 Pettingale brothers on page 34

FLITCHAM

GIFTS TO Lynn HOSPITAL. - Mrs. R. E. Wilson has received the following letter from the Matron of the Lynn Hospital:-

"Dear Madam, Thank you so much for your most welcome gift of nightgowns and red jackets. Sister and I were talking over our worn-out nightgowns, which really must be condemned, and we are so thankful to get a fresh supply. They are so well-made, too. Please tell your working party nothing could have been more opportune than their parcel. Yours faithfully,

(Signed) Helen Swain, Matron."

GAYTON THORPE & EAST WALTON

On Tuesday, Dec. 21st, the rector took three lads - Bland, Copeman and West - into Lynn to hear a lecture on birds, illustrated by cinematograph slides. Lady ffolkes gave the prizes to those children who had written good essays on Birds and Trees. We hope to get some prizes next year.

LITTLE MASSINGHAM

Another message to the parish reaches us from Canada. "Kindly convey to our many kind friends at Little Massingham hearty good wishes from us all at Massingham Ranch."

We are glad to get good news of Mr. and Mrs. Knights and their family. They have built their house. A School has been started in the neighbourhood since their arrival, to which they contribute several scholars. They have still to go four miles to church, but they have found that their clergyman the Rev. C. W. Peck was a former Lynn Curate. A new railway connecting with the trunk line at Calgary is about to be made, passing through their ranch, and this will be a source of great convenience to them. Altogether they speak very hopefully, but they have still to get through their first long cold winter.

WOLFERTON

His Majesty The King is making considerable alterations to the school buildings, which will be for the greater comfort of the children, especially the infants.

ANMER

ANMER has suffered from a severe epidemic of influenza during these last few weeks. Scarcely a house in the parish has been free from sickness.

Mrs. Dyble the oldest inhabitant of our little community has gone to her long rest: and nearly the youngest member has been taken thus early from the evil to come. Mrs. Dyble, who was born at Hillington, belonged to a long-lived and hardy stock.

Born in the year of the Battle of Waterloo, she has lived under five Sovereigns of Great Britain, and it was a great joy to her in her old age to have the privilege of meeting His present Majesty King Edward. Few will easily forget their Majesties' kindly interest and sympathy, for their old subject's fervent prayer for God's blessing upon them.

Mrs. Dyble for many years followed the old and honourable calling of a Midwife, and her kindness and skill in attending gratis on her poorer neighbours will long be remembered, together with her success in her attendance on her richer clients. She was called to her long home by GOD Almighty while still in the full possession of all her faculties. She lies - all that is mortal of her - in Anmer churchyard.

GAYTON THORPE & EAST WALTON

I omitted to note, in the March number, the death of one who had long lived at E.W., though she died at Gayton - Ann Curl, who passed away at the ripe old age of 84.

Amongst the rough, very rough and crude sketches, with which I do try occasionally attempt to illustrate events recorded in my private diary, are two; one, of a group in Walton church, showing Ann Curl, in a gorgeous bonnet, my youngest daughter, and her nurse. The child in a very audible voice, said, *"Nanna, look at Ann Curl's bonnet."* The other pictured old Grannie Jackson, Ann and myself, sitting round the fire in Grannie's cottage, with a huge kettle hanging over the fire, and containing some very succulent pottage. So it is possible that, in years to come, we shall all three - not to say five - be recalled in history, by those yet unborn. Such is greatness!!

Little did he know!

"Nanna" was the name of a child's nurse, not a grandmother. Ed.

The other day the rector was asked for, and supplied, a certificate of birth of one born in Thorpe 95 years ago!!! The old lady (whose maiden name was Loades) is still enjoying good health. May she be spared, with all her faculties in play, to join the ranks of the centenarians.

1910

GRIMSTON

Our death roll last month consists of four of our oldest inhabitants, all of the last generation, all of whom too had finished their active life for several years. Three of them had spent the last years of their life in our Union Workhouse, receiving there, we acknowledge thankfully, every consideration and kindness.

Still, we may hope that the day may come when all life's workers who, like these men, have done good work in their day and generation, may in their declining years enjoy the comfort of passing their last years in their own homes, or in the homes of their sons and daughters. It doesn't seem quite right that it should even be possible to be otherwise. Towards this our Old Age Pensions will, let us hope, in time lead us. Probably but for the very cruel disqualification which at present deprives the most really needy from pensions, these men would have found resting places in their native village for their last days.

Still this is of little consequence now. Their time of full rest has come, as it will come to all of us. May they rest in peace: and may the present generation of men and women fulfil their part in the world's great workshop.

"Man goeth forth to his labour and to his work until the evening."

NORTH WOOTTON

THE past winter has been a sad one for the parish in many ways. Grave sin has been common amongst us and indifference to religion appears to be increasing. Fewer people attend Church than a year ago. To many of us all this is a real sorrow, I feel sure. The way to remedy it is to cast ourselves more completely upon God, and to use every opportunity we have of bringing back again those of our relatives and friends who, at any rate for a time, have chosen to turn their backs on God. May God, in His infinite mercy, bring all of us to see and know our own sins - *as He sees and knows them!* And then may we all be led to a real repentance!

ANMER

THE month of May alas will be long remembered! The whole Empire mourns the loss of our great and good King Edward. The whole Empire, on Friday, May 20th, united to do honour to the great dead. We, not only as loyal and loving subjects, but as grateful neighbours and tenants, paid our simple but wholehearted tribute to his memory. Perhaps here, it was not his greatness, his unique position in the world, that we thought of so much as the familiar face, the genial and ever courteous manner, the gracious kindly act, which we are to see no more amongst us. It is the human personal side of that greatest of

PARISH MAGAZINE.

1910

England's Kings which we were privileged to see, and the loss of which, so sudden and so unexpected, touches us right deep down in our hearts. Our feelings are almost too deep for words, we know what we feel, but like all Englishmen, we find it difficult to express it publicly: lest those who knew him less well might think us insincere. Suffice it to say that we have lost a friend, and we know it. Friday May 20th, proved it to us here! At the Holy Communion at 7.30 - at Mattins at 10 - at the Memorial Service at 2.30 - at Evensong at 6.30, - there were real mourners.

During the day 187 were at these Services out of a population which all told is scarcely 200. Instead of sending one more wreath to the almost countless numbers which reached Windsor, it was thought better to send an offering to the King's Lynn Hospital, knowing how great was the interest that our King took in the work of alleviating sickness and suffering. Lastly, as we sang on Friday, we say again -

FATHER, in Thy gracious keeping
Leave we now Thy servant sleeping.

P.S. We feel that other matters must stand over to next month's Magazine.

CASTLE RISING & ROYDON

We at Castle Rising and Roydon have lost a kind neighbour as well as a King, and his removal leaves a blank in our local circle and life. His connection with Castle Rising dates back for a considerable time. For the last twenty-two years in succession he had been the guest of Lord Farquhar at the Hall, his visits lasting generally for the inside of the week, previously to that he had the shooting on the Estate for several years. By his kingly manner and kindly condescension he won the hearts of all. May he rest in peace.

Our sympathies go out to Her Majesty The Queen Mother, to His Majesty King George, and to all the Royal family in their bereavement.

Our loyalty is transferred to the new King, and our earnest prayer for him is that he may have strength and courage to cope with the responsibilities of his high calling.

ASHWICKEN

MEMORIAL SERVICE. - On Friday, May 20th, a Service in memory of our late beloved and lamented Sovereign Lord King Edward was held in the church at 1.30. The large number present showed how keenly the loss of our King was felt, and a loving desire to pay respect to his memory. Form II. of the appointed services was used, followed by a sermon preached by the Rector, who took for his text Psalm XLI. 1, "Blessed is the man that considereth the poor and needy, the Lord shall deliver him in the time of trouble." At the conclusion of the Service the "Dead March in Saul" was played by Miss Owen with all due solemnity and pathos.

ANMER

IT was with great surprise that on opening last month's magazine I found no Anmer news. I am afraid it must be accounted for by my being away and thinking of other things, at the time when it ought to have been written. I offer many apologies in this number.

HILLINGTON

THE Sandringham detachment of the Territorials marched through Hillington on July 30th, quite enlivening us with the strains of their band. At the station they were joined by the Hillington and Flitcham members, and went by special train to Norwich, where they camped out on Mousehold Heath. On Saturday, Aug. 6th, they returned, having had fine weather, hard work, a good time, and looking all the fitter for their week's strenuous soldiering.

GRIMSTON

NURSING CLASSES. - The two courses for women have now been taken. In the first course – 'First aid to the injured' - 21 - all, that is, who entered for the examination - successfully passed. In the second course – 'Home Nursing' - of the 17 who entered, 15 passed. This is a very satisfactory result. We shall all feel what an advantage to the community it must be to have now so many really qualified to give aid

THE MISSIONARY EXHIBITION.

THE Railway Companies offer to issue cheap tickets to Lynn, at the rate of a fare and a quarter for the double journey, on any of the eight days of the Exhibition, from Tuesday, September 20th, to Wednesday the 28th, to any person producing a ticket of admission to the Exhibition. Prominent notices will be posted up in each village stating where those tickets may be obtained. The price for the tickets will be 6d on Wednesday and Saturday, and on other days after 5 o'clock. On those days from 2 to 5, 1/-, and on the opening day 2/-. Children under 14 in all cases half-price. For Associations or Classes, arranged through a leader, the charge will be 4d per person.

So many persons go into Lynn between harvest and Michaelmas, that it is hoped that these facilities to the Railway Companies, dependent upon Exhibition tickets, will induce large numbers to purchase them - and we feel quite confident that all who take the opportunity of seeing the remarkable set of things which are being brought together, and hear the descriptions about them from the missionaries and others who will be ready to explain them, will find themselves taking quite a new interest in the cause of Foreign Missions.

in cases of accident amongst us.

As for the actual results of the examinations, this means that those who have passed both examinations are qualified to act, and indeed liable to be called upon, in the event of an invasion of this country by a foreign enemy. This we pray will never come to pass; but it is well to be prepared for such an event, and should it come, the call will be indeed urgent for skilled nurses.

Courses for men are to be arranged for the Autumn. We hope very much that there will be plenty of entries and that in the results the men will not be behind the women.

GRIMSTON

Amongst the 7,000 Laurel or evergreen wreaths that were sent to decorate the streets on the day of The King's funeral was one from Grimston.

GAYTON THORPE & EAST WALTON

We regret to record an accident to our young friend, Reuben Alcock. It is now a month ago and longer, since he fell from his bicycle when going to a cricket match, and injured his arm. This fall resulted in blood poisoning. The rector saw him the other day in Lynn Hospital, and where he seemed very bright. N.B. He was just going to have his dinner!! Now hereby hangs a moral. It was more than a month before the rector *heard* a word of the accident, although he must have been in the village two or three times every week, and naturally enough the lad's mother was surprised at his not calling to enquire. It would be a great help to, and is much desired by, all pastors in their parishes, if neighbours were to tell them of all cases of sickness.

Over and over again has the writer emphasised this fact. Pointer *dogs* can scent out *birds,* though they see them not "in cover," but no such gift is granted to human beings, and the parson is very human after all. Do help, my friends, in this matter!

ON Thursday, August 11th, 15 mothers, with Phyllis Burton and Alice Green, went off "on their own hook" to Snettisham beach, hiring a conveyance from Mr. Eagle of Castle Acre. They had a most gloriously fine day, and much enjoyed themselves. One incident in the day's doings gave an extra zest to the outing viz., a capital glimpse of the good Queen Mother and her sister, the Dowager Empress of Russia, AND the little dog Caesar.

IT will have been seen that in the last month it has rained rain, it has also rained trips.

NORTH WOOTTON

RETREAT FOR CLERGY. - Beginning on Monday, Oct. 10th, and ending on Oct. 14th, a Retreat for clergyman is to be held at Blakeney. Some 35 or 40 hope to be present at it, and I am looking forward to being one of the number.

A Retreat is a special time of more or less *unbroken* prayer, devotional reading and communion with God. As a rule there is no talking during the whole of the Retreat, except on certain special subjects, and this is only allowed during a certain part of each day. Many of you will, I feel sure, understand how blessed a time a retreat can be for those who go to it. It is especially important that parish priests should from time to time retire in this way from their ordinary lives, and spend some days in silent prayer, self-examination and thought. The parishioners are sure to be the gainers from any good that may come to their clergyman as the result of his going to a Retreat.

Will you pray for those of us who are hoping to go, and especially for him who is to conduct and lead us in our devotions?

ASHWICKEN

SOCIETY FOR PROMOTING CHRISTIANITY AMONGST THE JEWS. - On Sunday, Nov. 13th, sermons on behalf of the Jews Society were preached in our church at both services; in the morning by the Rev. H. H. Ashley Nash, and in the afternoon by the Rector, the total amount collected being just £1. There is much reason for regret that the result should be so meagre, especially when it is known as a fact that half of that amount was contributed by one person. Surely as members of the Church of Christ, we should remember that it is our duty, and should be our privilege, to do the utmost we can, and not the least, to further missionary work, and first of all that work which aims at the gathering in to the fold of Christ His own brethren.

May God pardon the coldness of our heart in the past, and stimulate us to greater efforts, and a much deeper sense of gratitude and responsibility in the future.

GRIMSTON

APPLICATION for 18 new pensions have been made at the Grimston Post Office to come into force on the 1st of January. The total of the ages of these candidates amounts to 1406 years, giving an average for each of over 78 years. This speaks well for the longevity of Grimstonians. The age of the oldest is 94. May they all enjoy this too long deferred boon for many years to come.

1910

CASTLE RISING & ROYDON

THE house-to-house collection for the West Norfolk and Lynn Hospital has again been undertaken by Dorothy Everett, and a sum of £1/18/0 been paid to the bank. This amount is a slight increase on last year's collection, but there are still a few houses who omit to add their small share to the support of this excellent institution.

WESTACRE

Mrs. Softly, the Postmistress of Westacre, was laid to rest on Oct. 26th, in the village churchyard. Her long illness was borne with great patience. Her husband and ten children followed her, in fact nearly all the village seemed to he represented at her funeral, whose presence testified to the great respect in which she was held.

THE choir desire to thank the many friends who so kindly contributed to the fund which gave them so enjoyable a treat last month.

_____

A RUMMAGE Sale was held in the parish room on the 19th, and a sum of over £9 was made towards the Nursing Fund.

WOLFERTON

THE sum of 13/6 has been forwarded to Dr. Barnardo's Homes as the result of a collection by the school children. The collectors were Sarah Batterbee, Maud Gent, Hilda Sayer and Stanley Hudson.

_____

THE school children contributed 3/- to the Memorial Fund to His late Majesty King Edward VII, and this has been sent to the Norfolk Education Committee.

Grimston Police Station 1910   *(Rev. W. Howard)*

(Rev. W. Howard)

Pott Row Green, Grimston. Approx. 1910. Old school house in background, now the Club room. Clock tower now demolished.

(Rev. W. Howard)

Corner of Pott Row Green and St. Luke's Church (Demolished approx 1970)

Lt. Massingham 1908 - All the villagers turned out to wish the Knights family well, before they left for Canada.

Lt. Massingham Rectory group leaving for a cycle ride - c1910   *(R. Jewers)*

The old rectory at Lt. Massingham c1910 (Demolished 1950s)   *(R. Jewers)*

The station at Lt. Massingham c1908 *(R. Jewers)*

(Castle Rising History Group)

5 of the Pettingale brothers. All lived in Castle Rising and worked on the Howard estate. Taken outside the Black Horse 1909.

Westacre new church clock installed in 1909

(T. Jewers)

34

PARISH MAGAZINE.
1912

It has not been possible to find a 1911 Parish Magazine that we could copy. Ed.

NARBOROUGH & NARFORD

Narborough and District Nursing Association held their Annual General Meeting in the Church Cottage, at 3 p.m., on Thursday, 25th January 1912. The following is the Statement of Accounts for the past year, viz: 1911.

Nurse's Salary for the year was: £52. 16s. 0d.

Laundress was £ 2. 8s. 0d.

Forty-seven cases were attended during the year, of which 17 were Maternity cases, the Nurse paying 460 visits in all. It is earnestly requested that when the Nurse is sent for, the nature of the case should be stated at the time, in order that she may be prepared with what is necessary.

The Harmonium that Nurse Brazier bought with money sent to her, as a private gift, from the Church Army Head Quarters, has been a great service in her voluntary work with her girls' classes in her cottage. There are 40 subscribers in Narborough, 42 in Pentney, 41 in Bilney, and 25 in East Winch; in future, Narford will be included.

WESTACRE

Easter Vestry Meeting. There were 17 present at this Meeting which was held on Wednesday, April 10th, at 8 p.m. Mr. Lewis was elected Vicar's Warden in the place of Mr. Wellingham who has left the parish, after many years valuable work for the Church. Mr. Joshua Reynolds was re-elected People's Warden, and Messrs. Brown, Fryer, Fuller and Holden were re-elected Sidesmen. After the business had been transacted, the Vicar was asked, on behalf of the parishioners, to present to Mr. John Reynolds a small testimonial of their appreciation of his services as Parish Clerk for 35 years. The presentation consisted of a Bible, Prayer Book, Clock and Pipe.

A Sexton and Grave-digger will, in future, take the place of the Parish Clerk, it will be an annual appointment, and Mr. F. Sculpher has been chosen by the Vicar and Churchwardens to fill this position for the ensuing year.

NARBOROUGH&NARFORD

The whole village received a great shock on that sad Monday in July when the news was passed from mouth to mouth that Mr. Wilson had been suddenly called away from this life whilst watching his hay-makers at their work. He was a gentle mannered, gentle minded man who had gained the regard of all his neighbours.

NOTE. - It should be noticed that the recently baptised Infant will bear, amongst his Christian names, that of "Rogers." This is a most marked testimony, paid by the child's parents, to the memory of their late Rector, the Rev. H. C. Rogers. Personally this has struck me as an exceedingly touching episode, and it gave me the most unqualified pleasure to "name this child" after my predecessor, old friend and neighbour.

WESTACRE

Repair of the Organ. For a long time we have felt that something must be done about the Organ.

After some 35 years service it is showing signs of wear, the bellows are worn out and a great deal of the mechanism requires attention. The gentleman who originally procured the instrument for the Church, and is himself acquainted with the nature of Organs, has advised us not to procure a new one but to have the present one thoroughly repaired and added to, as its tone and balance is very good. This will necessitate an expenditure of at least £40, and we propose to raise the sum by means of Concerts in the Winter and a Sale of Work in the early Summer. If everyone who is interested in our Church will do a little to help, there ought to be no difficulty whatever in getting the money. And so we should all take our share in providing an instrument more worthy to assist in the service of God.

NARBOROUGH & NARFORD

The Narford Mystery. Alas! instead of satisfying our readers' curiosity, which was perhaps excited by the last paragraph in

our November Magazine, I have to write of the very sad and mysterious disappearance of Ellen Shingfield.

She has been described to me, (for I did not know her), as a very quiet, well mannered, modest, attractive girl. Here is the story - a broken, jerky story, divided into several disconnected incidents.

On October 28th Ellen left Swaffham, and walked to Gt. Massingham. Why would she go to Massingham, no one seems to know. Offered shelter by a kindly couple, she slept that night under their roof, and then, with a Mrs. Tooke - known well by the way to me, as she was for some time one of my old parishioners – Ellen went towards Gayton and there, she seems to have been swallowed up as by some earthquake, for not a single trace of her has since been found - not one from that day to this, and I write on November 24th.

Surely the hearts of all kindly folk must go out towards the poor child, for she is not much more than a child - not yet seventeen. Poor motherless girl! I cannot dismiss the thought of her from my mind - she haunts my memory day after day and almost hour after hour. What has happened?

Mrs. Gayford, of Southacre, has done much to press enquiries, and I too have interviewed the Chief Constable of Lynn and, the Inspector in Swaffham, and twice written to Major Napier, the Chief Constable of the County. Can anything more be done? May God, of His mercy and goodness, disclose to us the truth of this distressing mystery. Whatever it be, may we know the truth about the girl.

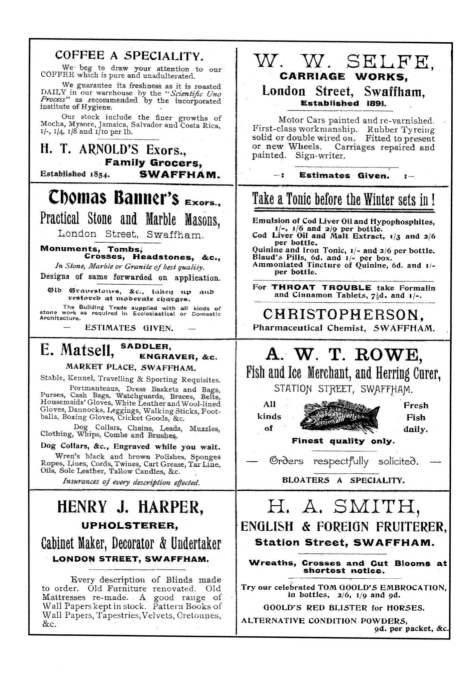
38

NARBOROUGH & NARFORD

HOLY BAPTISM.

On January 19th, 1913, at All Saints, Narborough, by the Vicar, Maurice Henry, son of Jesse and Lydia Dixon. [Born 18th November, 1912].

NOTE. - The above Baptism happened to fall on a Sunday Morning's Service. Although I most heartily welcome the bringing Children to Holy Baptism *"after the 2nd Lesson,"* at a Service *"when the most number of people come together"* (as the Rubric enjoins) yet the selection of a Sunday Morning should be regarded as *not a convenient time* for this Service, but rather as quite an exception to the general Rule. The Evening Service or the Children's Service should be selected.

Accidents will happen! One of our neighbours (a Sidesman to boot), Mr. Arthur Haverson lately met with a very nasty fall. Crossing the plank over the fleet in the early hours of a very dark morning, he fell, and catching his chin against the edge of the wood, sustained a fractured jaw. But for the aid of a young man, who was in his company, the result might have been much more serious, possibly fatal. By the way - permit me here a personal narrative:- After I had broken 4 or 5 limbs, at various times, I broke yet another. One neighbour accosting another said - "Have you heard the news? "No Bor! What's ter be?" "Why! our parson's met with *another Fatal* accident"!!

The 1st N.I.C. Members of The 1st Norfolk Imperial Cadets gave a capital Entertainment on Monday, February 17th, in the Foresters' Hall. Some folk insist on speaking of these young Patriots as a **"Corpse."** A great mistake - grammatical and personal - for these youngsters are very much alive, loyal to the very *core* of their being, they well deserve to be spoken of as a **"Corps."** I am told these cadets are betwixt and between Boy Scouts and the Territorials. Whatever they may be, they are certainly a very praiseworthy set of youngsters.

The Cadets gave a very well acted Farce, entitled - "The Pheasants' Eggs." There were Poachers and Gamekeepers and Police men and Cadets sometimes all of a heap and a pretty village lass, who was threatened by the poachers and rescued by the Cadets. Then there was a blood-thirsty murder, which turned out to be no murder and the upshot of it all was that vice was punished and virtue rewarded, and the Cadets forged to the front as a worthy Corps, alive and alert and deserving of all the support we can offer them.

Lastly! This piece de resistance was staged and brought to its most successful issue through the indefatigable efforts of Miss Bright-Betton and Miss Winnie Youngman of Bilney, to whom I, with all my readers, take off our hats or make our courtesies.

"God Save the King."

BURIAL.

On March 13th, 1913, the lingering illness of Mrs. Cropley, who had been blind for some few years, and was tenderly nursed by her daughter, was doubtless a relief to a great sufferer. It was a strange link with old friends for me to see round her grave the Walton faces of her nearest relatives. Some time after the Service I took down the names and messages written on the crosses and wreaths which covered the grave, but I am unable now to decipher many of them, as my writing was blurred by the rain. Suffice it then to say that many beautiful floral offerings were sent in memory of a wife, mother, grandmother and friend.

NOTE. - In connection with this Burial a remarkable incident occurred, which, at my request, the Rector of Southacre, who is well known as a Naturalist, kindly sent to the Daily Press. It will however bear insertion in our Magazine. The Sexton began the grave early and did not leave off his work until it was finished. Just two hours afterwards he returned to the churchyard and at once drew my attention to a nearly finished nest which two robins had built in a hole on the inside of the grave, caused by the falling of a large flint. Madame Redbreast must have been in such a hurry to provide furnished apartments for her eggs that there was little time for the careful selection of a site and the building of the moss-lined mansion. Pressing need sharpens the wits and quickens the efforts alike of birds and men.

NOTE. - It has been a touching and pleasing sight to mark how many graves have been covered with flowers this Easter-tide. There is no more appropriate way of marking our *lasting* affection for our dead than to tend their graves and turn them into gardens, and to garland them occasionally with beautiful flowers.

Burial Fees. The legal fee is 5/- for adult, 2/6 for child, but, as a general rule, the full fee is not insisted on, and only the 2/6 charged.

The Nursing Association. Mrs. Philip Gurney wishes to remind subscribers that they are entitled to the services of the Nurse, free of charge, excepting (A) - in Maternity Cases, when the fees remain the same as hitherto, viz: - 10/- and 17/-; and (B) - when the Nurse has to stay a whole night or day watching a case and then the charge of sixpence (6d.) will be made.

PARISH MAGAZINE.
1913 -1914

Narford Church. On Sunday, June 8th, I read the XXXIX Articles in S. Mary's Church, with certain comments on certain Articles. There was a large congregation. The Services will be at 3.15 p.m. until further notice. I have purchased 30 chairs and as soon as we are able to make the roof watertight and have got rid of the bees, I propose to return, to their proper place, the handsome Oak Seats which, the better to preserve them, have found a temporary home in Narborough Church. In future I hope to have Narford children baptized and Narford Brides married in Narford Church, as is fitting. The Church is yours, ye Narford folk, and I trust you will make full use of it.

WESTACRE

A Maypole has been provided for the School through the combined effort of the children, teachers and a few friends, to take the place of the one kindly lent by Heacham. It has been made by Mr. Fred. Overton, and the children hope to use it, for the first time in public, Friday, the 19th, when all parishioners are cordially invited to attend the Entertainment.

1914

NARBOROUGH & NARFORD

A Correction. I am told by discerning folk that my writing cannot be correctly described as "Calligraphy" (see Dictionary), for it is "shocking bad." Be this as it may, in the February issue, "Enterpe Polymna" should read - as you all will recognize - "Enterpe Polymnia."

Nursing Association. Our indefatigable and valued Secretary and Treasurer, Mrs. Philip Gurney, has issued her Annual Report for 1913. Nurse Brazier has paid 447 visits, attended 18 Confinements and 61 cases of general illness. For this she was accorded a vote of thanks and a Bonus of £2. The Doctor's fees were paid for 2 members, and the year's Finances showed a Deficit of £4. 7s. 2d. As Chairman (at the largely attended meeting when these details were announced) I proposed a vote of thanks - unanimously carried - to Mrs. Gurney, with a pleasing anticipation of her further help in the days to come.

Wanted!! Your late Rector used to put up, in the Porch, a list of things wanted for the Church. I follow his example, and name the following: -

(1) - **"A fair white Linen Cloth" for the Lord's Table.** (2) - **"Two coloured Burses and Veils" to cover the Holy Vessels, one**

41

Purple and the other Red. This will complete the set, as we have the green and white ones. (4) – "A Glass Cruet" for water for cleansing the vessels after use; and lastly, yet above all, the Choir Cassocks cry for attention! Some are in rags! This is a large order, it needs facing.

The Vicarage Sewing Meeting flourishes at the Vicarage.

WESTACRE

On Tuesday, February 10th, under the directions of the C.E.M.S., a well attended Meeting took place in the School, when the Rev. C. P. Hines, Head-master of Saham College; and the Rev. Dr. Kirkby, Rector of Saham, explained the position of the Welsh Church in regards to the Disestablishment Bill. So clear were the facts that we were able to realize the terrible blow the passing of the Bill would come to all Christianity in the Country.

At the close of the, Meeting a resolution, condemning the Bill, was read, we are glad to hear that a great number of signatures have been subscribed to the petition.

NARBOROUGH & NARFORD

Note. - We all are following our sailors and soldiers in their acts of patriotism, and I cannot but think other young men would do a thousand times better by following in the footsteps of their fellows than by remaining at home.

Let me emphasize what I have just said by the following very remarkable incident. The Rev. W. Emery Barnes, Halsean Professor of Divinity and Lecturer at Cambridge University, has written thus:

"In about 5 weeks the October Term begins.......I hope to meet in my Lecture-room no man between 20 and 30, who can pass the medical test, who has not offered himself for active service or ....for military training. There is a time for everything, and the present ....is a time for bearing arms ....The example set the country is not yet perfect."

Sunday School Treat. The Scholars and Teachers, mustering 50 all told, were invited by Mr. Dupuis to the Hall, and there entertained to Tea by Mrs. Dupuis. Games in the Park were enjoyed, especially a Cricket Match - English versus Germans, in which the British won by 7 runs.

The War. "To pray is to Fight." "To labour is to pray," said many of the laity in olden days. "To pray is to labour," retorted the good monks and nuns. And both were right. And we shall not be wrong, we stay - at - home - folk, if we take for our motto today the one heading this paragraph, since for us to pray is for us to fight. Its our special work. "We, like Moses, will tire at times, yet we've got to

PARISH MAGAZINE.
1914

go on praying! There are bound to be reverses, yet we must not waver. Our cause is just, and we may pray for victory since the war was none of our seeking. Our country expects that we shall, in these dire hours of trial, do our duty in the front praying-line. Let her not be disappointed.

NOTE. It has been suggested, from several quarters, that the hour of Noon shall be marked by the tolling of a Church Bell in every parish, calling upon all within sound of it to pause and say a **"Paster Noster"** or some short Collect, On behalf of our sailors, soldiers and allies. The bell rung at our own daily service will answer the same purpose, and when I happen to be away it shall be rung at Noon.

SOUTHACRE

Funeral - Edmund Thomas Daubeney, Rector of Southacre.

The Rev. E. T. Daubeney, whose body was laid to rest in the quiet Churchyard surrounding the Church he had served since 1904, was the eldest of a large number of brothers - by the way they were all well over six feet - all of whom were soldiers, he alone a parson, and the sons of Edmund Joseph Daubeney, Esq., J.P., of Cleeve House, Somerset, in the West Countree. At Oxford he played for the University at cricket, and was chiefly famed for his "slowtwisters." Graduating from Magdalene College, he was ordained in 1864 to the Curacy or Usk, and the next year became Rector or Bedhampton, Hants, where he spent 20 years, and then moved Eastward as Rector of Market Weston, near Thetford, and finally succeeded his own son, - probably an almost unique record - as Rector of Southacre. But, as was once remarked, the greatest conquest of his life was the winning of her who survives him and became the centre of a striking group of sons and daughters.

WESTACRE

During this terrible time of war our prayers are very earnestly desired for all in authority, and for the soldiers and sailors of our King. I do sincerely hope that every member of this parish will make it a rule to attend a place of worship on Sundays, and to remember, during their private prayers, all those in anxiety and need. By this time every house should have a copy of the Special Prayers issued by the Archbishops, and further copies may always be obtained by application to me. I am glad to be able to say that over £8. 10s. has been sent from the parish in response to the appeal of the Prince of Wales for the National Relief Fund.

PARISH MAGAZINE.
1915

WESTACRE

By the wish of the King and the Archbishops of Canterbury and York, Sunday, the 3rd, will be set apart as a day of Special Prayer and Intercession for the Nation. Let us, as a parish, respond to this great call to Prayer, believing that "where two or three are gathered together in Christ's name, there is He in the midst of them". The Services will be, as usual, at 11 a.m. and 6-30 p.m.

On Thursday, December 9th, a Meeting of the C.E.M.S. was held at the Mill House. A most interesting paper was read by Mr. White, of Swaffham, followed by discussion on the question - "Should wages be taxed?"

On Tuesday, December 22nd, at 2 p.m., the children of the Day School gave a bright little Entertainment to the parents and friends, and great credit is due to Mr. and Mrs. Brown and Miss Wiskerd for their careful training. The programme consisted of patriotic songs and old world dances which gave much pleasure to the audience as well as to the children themselves. At the end of the Entertainment a collection at the door realized £1. 8s. 11d., which, added to the contents of a box which had for a short period been placed in the Schoolroom, made up a sum of £1. 14s. which is to be sent to the Belgian Refugees.

In addition to this contribution it is worthy of record that the children have sent 18 pairs of mittens to those who are serving their Country from the parish, and 5/- to the Princess Mary Fund, besides that which was recorded in the December Magazine.

NARBOROUGH & NARFORD

The Christmas Gifts. The School Children were deluged with gifts just before Xmas. Spelman's Charity provided them with useful calico and delightful books, whilst Mrs. Herring, of Narborough House, once again presented the Sunday School Scholars with prizes such as their grand parents and even many of their parents never dreamt of in their young days.

School Treat. On Boxing Day, Mrs. Dupuis, of the Hall, gave a Tea to some 70 children of both parishes, with the Teachers and Choir Boys. After this, a Magic Lantern, lent and manipulated by the Vicar of Westacre (now also Rector of Southacre) threw a number of interesting and amusing slides, provided by Mrs. Dupuis, upon a sheet suspended in the Ballroom. The children returned to the servants' hall, where bran tubs, filled with presents, were dipped into, and the children were finally sent home rejoicing - laden with oranges and buns.

Mothers' Union. Mrs. Herring - that universal provider, gave, on the 29th, a Tea to the Narborough and Pentney mothers, who had crowded the Musick Room to overflowing, the residue going to the Dining-room. Then came a Magic Lantern in the Theatre, followed by a Play and a series of Living Pictures, illustrating some Nursery Rhymes. In these last, Mr. Philip Gurney's young people - born actors - and the children of Mr. Denny, most strikingly acted. The Play consisted of a talented cast of amateurs.

WESTACRE

Knitting Class. The members of Mrs. Clifford Wilson's Knitting Class have worked hard during the Autumn, and sent away the first parcel before Xmas. The parcel was sent to France to Dr. Munro, whose Motor Ambulances go daily from the Base Hospital to the Firing Line, and who gladly takes warm gifts and distributes them to men actually **in the trenches.** A very grateful letter of thanks has been received.

During last month two old parishioners and fellow workers on the late Mr. Tallent's farm passed away. For some five years James Reynolds had been terribly crippled with rheumatism. He bore his sufferings with splendid patience. Richard Andrews too was always hopeful that some day he might return to work, but God saw fit to take him somewhat suddenly at the end.

It is with great regret that I have been forced to abandon Special Week-day Services and addresses this Lent, because it is impossible to darken Church Windows and so comply with Police Regulations. I hope that the end message of preparation for Easter will not be forgotten, and that all of us will try to get nearer to God in our hearts at this solemn season.

NARBOROUGH & NARFORD
Our Sailors and Soldiers.

Commander Fountaine has been promoted to the rank of Captain. He is the youngest Captain in the Navy. I venture, though I know how modest he is, to add this much. A letter written to his parents, by a seaman on "The Lion," during the recent engagement, tells of the popularity of the Commander, and of the great trust the men have in him. But then, he is a Norfolk man, and one is reminded of what Norfolk men have done in the past; men such as Nelson, Blake and Troubridge, in the days of our old wooden ships of oak, and such as Wilson and Noel.

In the days of our iron-clads. Our Narford Squire bids fair to add to the long list of markedly capable Naval Officers belonging to the County. Though I have myself reached the old-age-pension of three-score-and-ten years, I hope to live to see our youngest Captain our youngest Admiral.

On 19th January 1915 the German Imperial Navy sent a Zeppelin L4 with the intention of bombing the Humber Estuary. The Captain mistook the North Norfolk coast for the Humber. However this did not stop him dropping several bombs in Norfolk.

They were dropped over Sheringham, Thornham, Brancaster, Hunstanton, Heacham, and Snettisham. The Zeppelin continued to King's Lynn where a further eight bombs were dropped. Two people were killed and many properties were wrecked. Some houses were badly damaged. The final bomb failed to detonate.

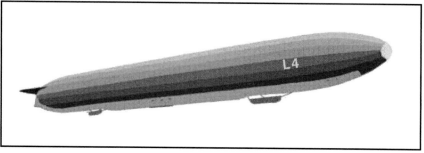

(R. Jewers)

Computer created picture of how the L4 Zeppelin may have looked

(Brian & Jan Gadd)

A crater 17' 6" (5.30 metres) wide, made by a bomb which just missed the Royal Train Shelter (background building) near to King's Lynn railway station.

(Brian & Jan Gadd)

Above:
Occupants being
evacuated from their
bombed house in
Bentinck Street

Left:
The Chief Constable
of King's Lynn
examining an
unexploded bomb

(Brian & Jan Gadd)

PARISH MAGAZINE.

1915

Private John Stevenson has been gazetted to a 2nd Lieutenancy in the Norfolks. I have also had a nice cheery letter from John Boughen, from the Front, to say he is now promoted to be Sergeant Major. Lance Corporal Holman has been raised to the rank of Sergeant, and was selected, out of many hundreds of others, for special duties, upon which he hopes shortly to enter. God bless our men and our dear lads, one and all, and bring them back to us safely at the close of this terrible war. Won't we give them a rousing welcome! NO FEAR!!

WESTACRE

Honour to Westacre: - We must congratulate Mr. and Mrs. Wright on having received the following letter from His Majesty the King:-

PRIVY PURSE OFFICE,
BUCKINGHAM PALACE, S.W.,
20th May, 1915.

Sir,

I am commanded by the King to convey to you an expression of His Majesty's appreciation of the patriotic spirit which has prompted your five sons to give their services at the present time to the Army.

The King was much gratified to hear of the manner in which they have so readily responded to the call of their sovereign and their country and I am to express to you and to them His Majesty's congratulations on having contributed in so full a measure to the great cause for which all the people of the British Empire are so bravely fighting.

I have the honour to be, Sir,
Your obedient Servant,

F. W. PONSONBY,
Keeper of the Privy Purse.

Mr. William Wright. Not only are Mr. Wright's five sons serving but be himself is a volunteer drilling at Castleacre every week.

The Bazaar. We may congratulate ourselves that the Bazaar in aid of the Organ Fund, and held in the Abbey Barn an unqualified success. Thanks to the kind and untiring work of many helpers, everything went off well, and we are only sorry that some were so tied to their posts that they lost much of the "Fun of the Fair." The pig, given by Messrs. Green & Kerridge, for which there was a great contest in bowling a ball through a hoop, was won by Mr. Everard after an exciting finish.

After the stalls were closed, dancing commenced, and everyone except the weary helpers seemed sorry when the strains of "God Save the King" from the excellent Massingham Band terminated the proceedings. The profit was £56. 2s.

CASTLEACRE

Church Services. Owing to the Lighting Orders, Evensong will be sung at 3.30 p.m. each Sunday until further notice.

PARISH MAGAZINE.
1915

For the Harvest Festival on 19th inst., the Church was prettily and tastefully decorated by the ladies of the parish. The collections amounted to £4. 9s. 8d., of which 3 guineas have been forwarded to the Lynn Hospital, and £1. 6s. 8d. to Swaffham Cottage Hospital.

On the 8th September the remains of Mr. Isaac Yallop, 61 years of age, who had died suddenly on the previous Sunday night, were laid to rest. As he had been a member of the local V.T.C., the coffin was preceded to the Church by the members, wearing their brassards, in charge of Sergeant Howard, Drill Instructor. Mr. F. G. Highe played appropriate Funeral Marches as the procession entered the Church and the Dead March as it left. "The Last Post" was sounded at the graveside.

Mr. Yallop had, for the last seven years, been employed at the Rectory, and his quiet and obliging manner had won for him many friends, who showed their respect in the many beautiful wreaths which were sent.

NARBOROUGH & NARFORD

East Anglian Field Ambulance. A special circular has been issued requesting the Clergy to notify to parishioners the great need there is for 100 more men to join the above Corps. Are there none here whose patriotism will lead them to respond to this call? I think I could put my finger on more than one man who might well respond thus to their Country's call.

RIFLE SHOOTING. The Rifle given by the Rev. F. K. Scott, the Vicar of Swaffham, for the best shot in the District Home Defence Corps, has been won by Mr. W. Denny, with a score of 85; Mr. Blake, of Narborough, and Mr, Ruscoe, of Castleacre, being 2nd and 3rd respectively. We are glad to think we have such deadly shots in our midst and feel all the safer for the fact.

CAMP TRAGEDY! On Tuesday an alarming tragedy stirred the whole of the higher end of the Camp. The Military Postman, who was sleeping in a small and hastily erected hut in the wood close to Mr Reeder's house, was burnt to death.

SEND-OFF. Between two and three hundred men from the Camp marched to Narborough Station, en route for Plymouth and the East, on Thursday, August 26th, amidst the cheers of onlookers and the hurrahs of the men themselves. Personally a wave of bitter anger against those very ambitious and cruel men, who are responsible for this wicked war, crossed my mind, but changed into intense pity for the lads - in the flower of their manhood - who were going to fight *"for England,*

Home and Beauty," since many a fine fellow amongst them may never see England again. And then, I found myself quoting the words - *"They shall beat their swords into plough-shares and the spears into pruning hooks, neither shall they learn war any more."*- Hasten that day, O Lord!!

NARFORD CHURCH. Steps are being taken to render the roof water-tight. I have also made some slight additions to the East end of the Chancel. We must crawl before we can walk, and walk before we can run. I hopefully look forward to the day when Narford Church will be one of the Show-Churches of the neighbourhood. It is quite capable of being so.

WESTACRE

Owing to the fact that no lights must be visible after sunset, it is necessary to alter the time of Evening Service. Consequently, during the winter months, the Service at Southacre will be at 2 o'clock, and at Westacre at 3.30. I fully realize that this is not a convenient time of day, but the exigencies of wartime give us no choice, and I do beg of our evening congregation to do their best to attend. Our congregations of late have been very small. In these days of anxiety and trouble, let us, at least on His Day, join together to commend our brave soldiers and sailors, as well as ourselves, into God's Hands.

NARBOROUGH & NARFORD

HOLY BAPTISMS.
Sept. 27th, 1915.
William Clifford, of Nottingham.
Sept. 27th, 1915.
Samuel Weston, of Nottingham.
Oct. 4th, 1915.
George Wilson, of Matlock.

NOTE. - The above three Baptisms were Adult Baptism, being soldiers in Narford Camp. The Sacrament, in each case, was administered by the Chaplain of the Forces, W. S. Hildesley, Brigade Chaplain, in Narford Church.

A Concert, given entirely by soldiers from the Narford Camp, on October 8th, was a most marked success. It was the best Village Concert I have ever heard and I shrewdly guess that more than one vocalist was a professional artist. Be this as it may, the whole programme went with a swing and without a flaw, and was altogether a treat to listen to. Had I not been bound to announce that there would be no encores, I am sure the concert would have taken just twice as long, for the spirit of the audience may be expressed in the words of the man, packed amongst the gods at some similar entertainment, who, when there was a shout of "Encore," drowned all the other voices by exclaiming – "Blow the Hencore! Let's have it again! !"

PARISH MAGAZINE.
1915

A Second Concert was given by the soldiers of Narford Camp, on October 22nd, as excellent in its details as that given on a previous occasion. We had this time the great advantage of having a lady at the piano, who also favoured us with one song. Her accompaniments were most efficient.

The whole Entertainments went without a hitch, thanks to the Master of Ceremonies – Lc. Corpl. Parkinson.

As Vicar, I expressed the thanks of the Narford people and of those of Narborough who attended the Concerts: to Colonel Herring, for twice lending us and erecting the Stage Scenery.

NOTE. **"It is a sweet and seemly thing to die for the Fatherland."** And Arthur Twiddy has done this - the first of our own lads, as I trust he may be only one. Nevertheless, since we must all die some day, and can only die once, what nobler death can a man die than that of fighting in a just and holy cause? To parody well known words, as applicable to this particular time:-

"Tis better to have fought and died
Than never to have fought at all."

Unless "starred," **as doubtless many can justly claim to be,** surely any one might well be ashamed to shirk behind the Voluntary System, whilst others are doing their duty. Fancy anyone replying to the famous signal of Lord Nelson in such terms as these: **"I shan't come unless I'm obliged! If they want me they'll have to come and fetch me!"**

It was with unqualified regret that I found it quite impossible to reach home in time to take the Service myself. However, I am thankful to my kind neighbour, the Rev. L. G. Titley, Rector of Southacre and Vicar of Westacre, for coming to my aid. Doubtless it will be a satisfaction to all the parish that Mr. Haydon, the lad's old School-master and Choir-master, kindly played "The Dead March," and that soldiers acted as bearers, and that the sad and solemn Service closed with "The Last Post." To all who mourn so early a death (and who does not) I would suggest the following passages of God's Word:- Phil. 1, 23; and I Cor., 2, 9.

We shall greatly miss those soldiers from the Choir and the congregation who so greatly help to brighten and swell the number of worshippers on Sunday evenings.

Note. - I hear that other men have volunteered during the last week to help - under God - to end this awful and wicked war by destroying the military despotism with which all Europe has been threatened by Prussian Militarism.

NARBOROUGH & NARFORD

Concerning Christmas Cheer. (1) - A Dinner to 30 soldiers. (2) - To 60 soldiers a Meat Tea. (3) - To all School Children a Tea, Magic Lantern and Presents from Old Father Xmas. (4) - To all the School Children, Books and Calico. (5) - Two head children in each class of Sunday Schools, specially beautiful Books. Surely I was not wrong in describing the parish as enjoying "a perfect surfeit" of Entertainments. All five came with a rush, tumbling over each other with the cry – "Here we are again," as the clown and the harlequin used to smother the Policeman when I was a boy at school 60 years ago.

The Sewing Meetings at Narborough House, consisting of the members of the Mothers' Union and Mrs. Herring's old Bible Class, are doing excellent work this season for the British Red Cross Society. Some 25 to 30 members sewing, others making lavender bags, &c., for the Hospitals.

In addition to this work before Xmas, a large number of scrap books were made at the meetings for a very poor parish in London, and various boys and girls, hearing from their mothers of the work being done, voluntarily contributed a great many made by themselves.

(Narborough Research Group)

Narborough Aerodrome 1918 drawn by Timothy O'Brien 1994

(Narborough Research Group)

40 Service Personnel were killed or died whilst at Narborough and Marham between 1916-1918. Nearly all were as a result of accidents whilst undergoing flight training.

Creator of Biggles - W. E. Johns was a flying instructor at Narborough in 1918. The Narborough Research Group book, 'The Great Government Aerodrome', notes his concerns at the time that spies could have been responsible for some of the 'plane accidents'.

1917 crash scene　　　　(The 'Liddle Collection', The University of Leeds)

(Narborough Research Group)

Handley Page V/1500 known as 'The Super Handley'

(Narborough Research Group)

Handley Page 0/400 (Known as The Bloody Paralyser)

WESTACRE
Letter from the Vicar:

My Dear Friends,

I feel I must write a few lines to tell you something of the work I have been allowed to take up during my absence from Westacre. I have been appointed as a Chaplain to a Military Hospital in a Garrison town. The population of my "Parish" consists of some 400 patients with a staff of Medical Officers and Nurses and 350 R.A.M.C. men. There is a beautiful little Chapel formed out of one of the Wards, where the Sunday Services consist of a Celebration of Holy Communion at 7 a.m., Parade Service at 11, and Evensong at 6. There is also a very fine Garrison Church standing on a hill in the centre of the town where I help in the Services on week days.

Life is a busy round, soldiers everywhere, and bands playing and bugles sounding continually. I am glad to say I have an old Westacre friend here, Driver E. Tuddenham, A.S.O., attached to the Field Ambulance. I do hope you will all remember me in your prayers, for there is much to be done and so many opportunities which must not be missed. I think often of all my friends in Westacre, and, like all the men, who are to do their bit, look forward to the time when the victory having been won, we can come home with light hearts, thankful for the privilege of having been allowed to do something, however small, for the old country and the old parish which we love so well.

I am,

Your affectionate friend and minister,

LIONEL G. TITLEY

NARBOROUGH & NARFORD
Entertainment to Soldiers.

"What! another! Yes! Yes! yet another, and why not?" Colonel and Mrs. Herring gave an Entertainment, at Narborough House, on Wednesday, January 26th, to a number of soldiers, some sixty in all. It would be equally correct to say that the soldiers had entertained their entertainers, as well as being themselves entertained.

To begin the evening the soldiers saw and enjoyed what, in my boyhood's days we used to describe as "A BUN DANCE ON THE TABLE." Then there were songs and a couple of "Curtain-Raisers," as I believe short Plays are now called. Anyhow, these examples of the Dramatic Act were certainly Cheer-raisers! Nor is this a matter of surprise, seeing that Miss Herring was "The Leading Lady," Miss Betton, "Mechanical Jane;" and Miss Etta Hutchinson, not only her own charming self, but also someone else no less charming. The Duets,

PARISH MAGAZINE.
1916

with piano and cornet accompaniments, by Sergt. Major Hulley, Corpl. Kelly and Pte. Platt, were given with much feeling and expression. Applauded and encored were Corpl. Kelly's most clear renderings of Solos on the Cornet. Pte. Marsden, from Bilney Red Cross Hospital, was quite first class as a comic reciter, bringing down the house - though not the roof - that we leave for Huns to attempt - with rounds of applause. Quarter-master Sergt. Stannard sang two songs no less enthusiastically acclaimed. In short, as a "Tommy" remarked "The whole show was a blooming success from start to finish." All thanks to our Host and Hostess. Nevertheless, as a true historian, I am bound to confess, that, after all, the evening's Entertainment ended in SMOKE!!

BURIAL.

On August. 9th, 1916. By the Vicar: John Billings, aged 67.

Note. - Very gradually his strength failed, and he passed away as though in sleep. There were several wreaths laid upon his grave, and I took down the senders' names to record them, and regret that I have mislaid the record. Universal sympathy will go out to Mrs. Billings in her great loneliness.

The Fete for the Nursing Fund proved a great success. Col. and Mrs. Herring threw open their delightful grounds and a large attendance of visitors caused the whole show to "hum" again. The entertainments were exceptionally good; the Tableau Vivant most touching.; the bran-tub most profitable; the tea devoured to the last crumb of cake and drop of bewitched water. The bowling greens and croquet lawns in constant use, and the Baby Show (headed by Master Fred Mays, at 1 stone 7 lbs. at six weeks old) was the delight of mothers, sisters and aunts. The Nursing Fund benefits by £51.

Narborough House and Narborough Vicarage have both entertained some of the inmates of the Red Cross Hospital, and let us hope the afternoons were enjoyed. More such, doubtless, will follow in due course.

For eight months, from November to July, the Vicarage Working Parties have continued every week, and during that time we have made and sent to a large hospital at the front line, the following garments: -
14 pairs pyjamas; 6 night-shirts; 3 helpless night-shirts; 14 pairs slippers; 2 pairs operation stockings; 84 body bandages (many tailed); 33 knee bandages; 4 operation pillows; 6 swabs; 2 pairs socks; 1 scarf. We have about 50 yards of flannel in hand.

HARVEST FESTIVAL.

Thanksgiving Services were held on S. Michael's Day and the

PARISH MAGAZINE.
1916 - 1917

Sunday following. On Friday the choir were strengthened by Volunteers from the R.F.C camp. The preacher was the Rev. E. H. Whall, Rector of N. Barsham. The collections amounted in all to £11. 15s., of which the R.F.C. Camp subscribed £3. 5s. 6d. Swaffham received £8, and Lynn £3. 15s.

I may add here, that during the absence of our people's warden on military service, Mr. Wellingham has kindly undertaken to act as his deputy.

___

My heart ached when visiting on October 13th, at Narford, a young Widow, with little ones at her side, who mourns the death in action, of her husband, Pte. J. A. Adams, one, of our most gallant, "Norfolks."

And then on October 14th I was distressed to hear that Pte. Edward Fawkes was killed on September 15th. A steadier lad, a more thoughtful, affectionate, and dutiful son (for several years the chief support of his mother), and physically a better set-up young Englishman it would be hard to find. R.I.P.

I trust we shall have good news after all of E. Twiddy, another nice Narborough lad. But the contemplation of the loss of the flower of our manhood is nothing less than appalling.

1917

NARBOROUGH & NARFORD

DISTRICT NURSING. - Mrs. Gurney's report at the Annual Meeting on Jan. 29th told us that the nurse visited 19 maternity, 36 surgical, and 42 medical cases, involving 1,463 calls. It is particularly requested that a written and not a verbal message be sent to the nurse where her services are required.

Receipts.- Balance, £2. 10s. 3d. General Subscriptions, £19. 16s. Members Subs, £19. 2s. 4d. Sales, £50. 18s. 4d. L. G. Grant, £3. 10s. Lynn Gardens, £3. Total, £98. 16s. 11d.

Expenses. - Nurses Salary: £54. 5s. 6d. Board, £6. 8s. Uniform, £3. 6s. 1d. Medical Expenses, £6. 11s. 1d. Extra Fees, £2. 18s. 8d. N.N.F. Fees, £1. 10s. Printing, &c., £1. 15s. 2d. Balance, £22. 2s. 5d. Total, £98. 16s. 11d.

Audited by Mr. Bristowe of Barclay's Bank, King's Lynn.

___

THE RED CROSS HOSPITAL.

The Annual Meeting synchronized with the official visit of the Government Inspector, who reported favourably:- Income, Donations and Subscriptions £188. 10s. 10d.

Church Offering, £13. 18s. 11d.
Entertainments, £130. 5s. 4d.
C. Grant, £10. Value of Gifts in hand, £70. 10s. 9d.
W.O. Grant, £1,111. 7s.
Total, £1,524. 12s. 10d.

Expenses:-
Deficit, 1916, £41. 5s 3d.
Maintenance and Equipment, £1478. 8s. 5d. Balance, £5. 1s. 4d.
Total, £1,524. 12s. 10d.

184 men admitted and 7043 beds made up during 1916, 63 admissions up to date, and 40 beds now occupied.

NARBOROUGH & NARFORD

RED CROSS HOSPITAL. - The Officers of R.F.C. very recently gave us a very pleasant musical evening in the Foresters' Hall, on behalf of the above object.

FOOD RESTRICTIONS. - The King's Proclamation was read by me in both parish Churches on Suns., May 6th and 13th, to which I endeavoured to add certain comments, alike timely and telling.

CASTLEACRE

BAPTISM. - Apl. 29th, Douglas Le Havre Walker.

BURIALS. - May 3rd, Zipporah Maclean, aged 88.

The Easter Vestry met on April 18th, when the accounts were being presented in due order; both "Church Expenses" and "Choir and Organist Fund" showed a diminished balance - but the thin congregations mean thin offertory bags.

The subject of the desecration of the Churchyard was discussed, and those who, for the sake of a few steps: repeatedly make fresh footpaths were censured. Every inch of "God's Acre" is sacred; what must He think of those who, with one breath, repeat:-

"Hallowed be Thy Name" - and with the next, scramble over the Churchyard walls and graves? This is sacrilege.

Our School has been closed owing to many cases of **German measles. Cannot this malady be re-named.**

NARBOROUGH & NARFORD

MARRIAGES IN WAR TIME. Glancing over the Narborough Banns Book I found that in the 15 years previous to my Incumbency there were 39 published and in the 5 years during my Incumbency we have had 38. Rather a remarkable contrast, I think.

R.F.C. - Lieutenant William Sutton Smeath, aged 22, was killed at the aerodrome the other day. His body now rests amongst his own people in Yorkshire. He gave his

PARISH MAGAZINE.
1917

life to his country and his soul is now at peace. Brother Officers tell me that he was a very promising aeronaut and a charming companion. - R.I.P.

THE SOLDIERS' GRAVES. - I have been frequently struck by noticing the bouquets of roses and flowers placed upon these five graves by unknown hands. Kindly hearts have honoured lads taken so suddenly from our midst. And shall let their friends know that this has been so.

RED CROSS HOSPITAL. - Thanks to the untiring energies of Mrs. Critchley-Martin, a Fete on Bank Holiday was held in the Hall grounds and proved a great attraction and success. Over a thousand tickets were sold.

CASTLEACRE

Pte. George Moore (Norfolks) is reported instantaneously killed in action. We offer much sympathy to his wife and child.

Upon his return from leave. Corpl. Stanley R.F.C., found a third stripe and a post at Headquarters awaiting him. Many congratulations!

The Sunday School Treat on Aug. 5th was very successful; games and competitions were admirably arranged by Messrs. Highe and Ruscoe, and others War-time refreshments took the place of the usual tea, and we all discovered that our enjoyment was just as keen. All went most merrily, and may we whisper that perhaps the experiences of our elders on the see-saw gave us the heartiest of all our laughs.

NARBOROUGH&NARFORD

Recent events seem almost to crush one. We have to record the death of a gallant lad, a good son, a studious scholar, a reverent chorister, John Jones, R.N., who went down in "The Recruit" when that ship was mined. John was a fine lad full of spirits, and giving great promise of rising in his self-chosen career. We trust that his mother may find in her boy and girl the comfort she could not fail to have found in her elder lad.

Then we mourn six losses in eight days, connected with the Aerodrome: Lt. W. H. Marshall - buried at Weston-super-Mare; Lt. Percy Gadon Shellington, 24 - buried by the Vicar of Marham, in our Churchyard; Lt. Edward Stuart Vaile, 23 - the elder son of the Rev. A. and Mrs. Vaile, of West House, Seaford, who went out as a despatch rider with the B.E.F. in Aug., 1914, and was gazetted in July last to the R.F.C., in which he became an instructor; Lt. Norman Victor Spears, 29, and his observer, Sidney Burrell. All this is very sad, and to many of us very puzzling. Why should this one be taken? Why should this one be left? Why should not both be left? And there is no answer, saving this – *"What I do thou knowest not now, but thou shall know hereafter."* Yet as we stand by the nine graves of these nine lads - for they were most of them but lads - we rejoice to know that they were "good lads." This is what I have heard from the lips of relatives and comrades, and so I seem to see a glimmer of light piercing the cloud and feel justified in applying the words of Solomon to *each* of these cases.

"Speedily was he taken away lest that wickedness should alter his understanding or deceit beguile his soul."

How Solemn was the sound of the last volleys; more solemn still "the Last Post," and what beautiful flowers were sent, not only by the nearest and dearest, but by Commanding Officers, Officers, Non commissioned Officers and brother Mechanics – to which I was glad in each case to find that Mrs. Crawford had added a home-made wreath.

A headstone has just been put over one of these graves, and the inscription runs thus : - In Loving Memory of Sec.-Lt. Allen Ingham Murphy, R.F.C.S.R., only son of Mrs. D. A. Murphy, Macdonald College, Prov. of Quebec, Canada. Killed on 31 March, 1917, in an aeroplane accident, aged 20. The head slab bears the R.F.C. badge.

CASTLEACRE

Sergt. H. J. Askew sends home this "parchment": "I have read with great pleasure the report of your Regimental Commander and Brigade Commander regarding your gallant conduct and devotion to duty in the field on Aug.11th, 1917, E. of Ypres. - R. R. Lee, Major-General." What an honoured treasure for his wife and 7 children (6 sons) !

"Our Day" surpassed all former ones: Castle Acre sent in £30. 4s.; Newton, £1. 8s. 5d.; South Acre, £4. 11s. 9d. How did we get it? Flag-selling; an afternoon fete with bazaar; fruit and vegetable, refreshment stalls; competitions; finding out our height and weight! All this to the accompaniment of a charming mandolin band. Outside there were wonderful 1d. dips for children AND grown-ups, and great delight for youngsters, having 1d. rides on the gaily decorated ponies. Then the Hall was packed full for an excellent concert, arranged by the generous "Flying men", who afterwards showed us their appreciation of an impromptu dance.

NARBOROUGH&NARFORD

NEWS OF OUR LADS. - *Lieutenant J. Stevenson* - has got his "pip" and has also left Egypt to join the Indian Army.

PARISH MAGAZINE.
1917 - 1918

Sergt. Major Boughen has been gazetted to a Sec. Lieutenant in R.F.A. Most heartily is he to be congratulated, for much active service has he seen for many years.

Herbert Watson has written many letters from the Front, and two of these I have been allowed to see. In one he speaks of a fight in which he encountered and overcame 15 Germans, after which his Company Captain entertained the men to a "ripping tea" and "the Spades" - a species of concert; and in the other he caps the story, for he tells us he has been awarded the Military Medal. This is the third Military Medal won by Narburians.

Albert Pitcher and *John Turner.* have been wounded. The former is in "Blighty" and "doing fine"; the latter hoping to be here soon, but not as yet "going strong."

We all must specially sympathise with Widow Turner, who has received so many blows during the last 4 years.

William Holman was married very recently (see below) and is soon to go out to Mombasa. From thence he travels by rail and road many hundreds of miles to Uganda. He tells me he has "been to school again," learning the language of the *Sudanese*. When he reaches his destination, he is to drill Sudanese troops composed of men of magnificent physique.

When "licked into shape" they have the credit of being as smart on parade as are our own Household Troops.

MARRIAGE. - On Nov. 3rd, 1917, at Gt. Ryburgh, *William Holman* and *Mabel Ely.*

NARFORD CHURCH. - I fear I shall have to ask the Bishop to allow me to close the Church during the winter months, as there is the very greatest difficulty to get coke, without which the necessarily fireless Church is, in its present sad state, alike damp, dank, and depressing.

Advent Wed. Afternoon Services had been arranged for, but have fallen through.

1918

CASTLEACRE

MARRIAGES. - Christmas Day Pte. L Jakes and Effie Wilmot. Boxing Day - Archer Bloy and Edith Mobbs.

Lce.Cpl. C. Savage, reported missing, is now officially announced to have been killed in action. Keen sympathy is felt for his relatives.

Elijah Bloy, R.N.D., is severely wounded, a second, time, to our great regret.

Our village is represented in many branches of the services:-

PARISH MAGAZINE.
1918

A. W. Barrett, having passed his examinations in wireless telegraphy, must now be addressed O.T.

___

Castle Acre is proud to provide West Acre a second time with an organist: the post, filled so ably for some years by W. Ward, has just been accepted by Abbey Taylor (pupil of Miss Highe), who thus at an early age has the privilege of devoting his musical talent to the glory and worship of God in His Church. Our best wishes speed him.

___

Miss Yates, N.C.C., gave us a most helpful and interesting lecture upon economical uses of potatoes in many ways. The small attendance was much regretted. So much was to be learnt by willing minds beyond the mere every-day *peeling* and boiling of our plentiful crops. Those who have made and eaten "potato butter" in these days of scarcity are grateful for that teaching alone. Can we learn too much in these ways?

___

SOLDIERS CHRISTMAS PARCELS

The sum of £49. 5s. was collected, under Mr. Ruscoe's organisation, for sending a parcel to every man from Castle Acre, Newton, and South Acre serving with the forces. £47. 6s. 5d. of this, has been expended in sending 150 presents, most of which have been acknowledged. A few still await correct present addresses.

Parcels sent abroad contained : - 1 tin baked beans, 1 tin sliced bacon, 1 tin sardines, 1 tin camp - pie or plum pudding, 1 plum cake, 20 cigarettes, ½lb. biscuits, ¼lb. chocolate.

Men serving in England received postal orders and cigarettes. There were 3 classes of recipients:
(1) Those abroad. (2) Those who *have* been abroad, (3) Those away from home, not having been abroad.

___

NARBOROUGH & NARFORD

YULE-TIDE. - On Xmas Day the communicants at Narborough were slightly above the average usual on this Festival. Narford Church is unfortunately and perforce - with the Bishop's consent - closed for a time.

ON S. STEPHEN'S DAY Mrs. Crawford and Mrs. Denny entertained the Hospital Soldiers in the Festival Hall, which was most generously lent them for the occasion. After tea there was a Whist Drive. The party broke up with mutual regrets.

ON NEW YEAR'S EVE Mrs. Herring, of Narborough House (aided by her daughters, Lady Seale and Mrs. Percy Boughey, and by Mrs. Harry Beale, Sir John and Capt. Seale) entertained the soldiers of the Hospital to a most scrumptious (a good word, this, though slangy) tea, followed by

PARISH MAGAZINE.
1918

that thrilling semi-comic tragedy "Mechanical Jane." The leading lady was impersonated by that accomplished and charming actress, Miss Muriel Bright-Bettin, and the two other characters by Mrs. Critchley-Martin and Miss E. Hutchinson. Everyone agreed that they had all had a good time.

WAR PICTURES. - The first of a series of these Pictures, presented to the Church by inmates of the Narborough Auxiliary Hospital, has been framed, and fastened to a selected pillar at the west end of the Church. There, I trust it will long remain to recall "The Great War."

A complete Roll of Honour will shortly appear in the Church Porch.

The monthly collection for the Red Cross Hospital was most successful :-

Mrs. Elsey	£1/4/9
Mrs Brown	1/6
Mr Pitcher	3/10½
Mrs Cresswell	5/7½
Total	£1/15/9.

CONGHAM

ON Sunday, Dec. 23rd, a Carol Service in aid of the National Institute for Blinded Soldiers was held in Congham Church. The Choir was augmented by many willing helpers from Grimston and Roydon. Violin Solos "Dreaming" *(Schuman)* and "Largo" *(Handel)* were played by Mr. Hubbard, of Appleton, and bass solos were sung by Mr. Sculpher, of Gayton. A very large congregation attended, and joined heartily in the special hymns. The collection amounted to £4/10.

FLITCHAM

FOUR war-time Cooking Lectures were given on the evenings of Jan. 14, 15, 16 and 17, in the kitchen of Harpley Dams House. Considering the weather these were well attended. All those present thoroughly appreciated the valuable hints and Miss Beaton is to be congratulated on the clearness with which she demonstrated.

WOLFERTON

THE children's Treat on Dec. 31st was much enjoyed, and thanks are due to those who contributed towards its cost. The children played games, and received two small presents each, besides crackers, buns and apples.

H.M. The Queen, accompanied by Princess Mary, visited the School on Jan. 14th, and gave each child with teacher a nice present.

THE sad death of little Willie Ringer came as a great shock to his school friends and teachers, as well as to his bereaved parents. The children attended his funeral, and sang "There's a friend for little children." They also purchased a very nice wreath for his grave.

The Rev. J. R. Crawford in his study at Narborough Vicarage

The Reverend John Crawford was vicar of Narborough and Narford between 1912-1924. His previous parish was East Walton. He has often been described as the "The village scribe of the Great War Years".

> *"His writings give an insight into rural life of the period and his eloquent and sensitive words express deep personal feelings about the tragic events that overtook the local community and the world at large. He died on 28th March 1924 in his 80th year and was buried at Narborough Churchyard."*   'THE GREAT GOVERNMENT AERODROME'

(Narborough Research Group Book)

No. 53 Training Squadron, RFC Narborough

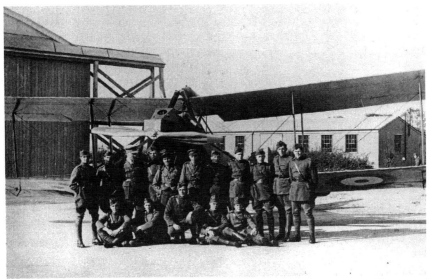

Members of No. 50 Reserve Squadron in front of an Armstrong Whitworth FK8 at Narborough in 1917. At this time they, and all personnel of the Royal Flying Corps (R.F.C.) wore khaki uniforms similar to army dress.

The Royal Air Force was formed on 1st April 1918 and a new uniform was gradually introduced designed for the R.A.F. in air force blue. Ranks were also changed i.e. the equivalent of an army Major was a Squadron Leader.

NARBOROUGH AERODROME
1915-1919

WEST NORFOLK'S FIRST AERODROME WAS OPENED IN NARBOROUGH PARISH IN AUGUST 1915, JUST OVER A MILE FROM THIS SPOT. IT GREW IN SIZE TO BECOME THE LARGEST ALL - AIRCRAFT AERODROME IN BRITAIN DURING THE FIRST WORLD WAR - ONLY FOUR AIRSHIP STATIONS COVERED A LARGER ACREAGE.

IT OPENED INITIALLY AS A NIGHT LANDING GROUND FOR THE ROYAL NAVAL AIR SERVICE, BUT SOON DEVELOPED INTO A ROYAL FLYING CORPS TRAINING STATION. IN APRIL 1918 THE AERODROME WAS TRANSFERRED TO THE NEWLY FORMED ROYAL AIR FORCE, AND AT THE SIGNING OF THE ARMISTICE NEARLY A THOUSAND SERVICE MEN AND WOMEN WERE BASED THERE. IN IT'S SHORT HISTORY, PERSONNEL INCLUDED BRITISH AND AMERICAN AIR AND GROUND CREWS, MEMBERS OF THE WOMENS AUXILIARY AIR CORPS (LATER, THE WOMENS ROYAL AIR FORCE) AND GERMAN PRISONERS OF WAR. W. E. JOHNS AND ALAN COBHAM WERE TWO OF A NUMBER OF WELL KNOWN PERSONALITIES WHO WERE STATIONED THERE.

TWENTY ONE SQUADRONS SERVED AT NARBOROUGH. TWO SQUADRONS, NOS 59 AND 121 FORMED AT THE STATION, ELEVEN WERE TRAINING OR RESERVE SQUADRONS, AND TWO, NO.35 AND NO.83 WERE FRONT LINE SQUADRONS. IN ADDITION THERE WERE THREE AMERICAN AERO SQUADRONS, AND AFTER THE WAR ENDED, THREE RETURNING CADRE SQUADRONS.

A LARGE NUMBER OF AIRCRAFT TYPES WERE IN SERVICE, RANGING FROM THE EARLY AVRO 504S, TO THE FE2BS, DH9S AND RE8S, SOPWITH CAMELS AND SNIPES.

THE AIRFIELD CLOSED IN 1919 AND THE LAND RETURNED TO AGRICULTURE.
NARBOROUGH LOCAL HISTORY SOCIETY 1996

NARBOROUGH AERODROME
1915 ~ 1919

This memorial is dedicated to the men and women who served at Narborough Aerodrome in

THE ROYAL NAVAL AIR SERVICE
THE ROYAL FLYING CORPS
THE ROYAL AIR FORCE
during the Great War 1914-1918
" LEST WE FORGET "
MCMXCVIII

These two plaques can be seen in Narborough Churchyard   *(T. Jewers)*

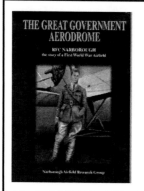

'THE GREAT GOVERNMENT AERODROME'

More information about the Narborough aerodrome can be found on page 136 Ed.

PARISH MAGAZINE.

1918

LITTLE MASSINGHAM

A COMPANY of Little Massingham Girl Guides has been formed, and have been working steadily all the Autumn. It will, we hope, do well in the New Year.

LETTERS have been received from our soldiers abroad and in England, expressing how they appreciated the parcels sent to them from Little Massingham for Christmas, and sending their thanks to those who so kindly provided them.

NORTH WOOTTON

OUR SOLDIERS. - Pte. R. F. Blake is home for his overseas leave. When he goes for service abroad he will carry with him the best of good wishes from us all, and our prayers for his safe return. Of Edward Overland no certain news can be obtained. Not since Oct. 18, 1916 has anything been received from him, and we can only believe he is no longer living. His life was very precious to *one* in North Wootton, and to her we offer our real sympathy, and also to his family and friends.

NORTH RUNCTON

William Batterbee is home again and we are glad to see him and congratulate him on his release from being a prisoner in Germany. He has had to lose his right arm and for this he deserves every sympathy. Sydney Rowe has been invalided home, and we wish him a speedy recovery from his sufferings. Lewis Berry was home a few days ago looking fit and well. Much sympathy is felt for Mr. and Mrs. Thurston whose son has been killed in action, and also for his wife. May God comfort their hearts.

WEST WINCH

Note. The Rev. W. T. Gifford was parson of West Winch and also an Army chaplain serving in several UK camps. Ed.

20th Feb. 1918.

My dear Friends,

To live in a place where things happen and not to be able to write anything about it that may be interesting, makes it hard to know what to write about. The things that are of most interest in our work we may not mention. All I can say is we chaplains get plenty of hard, but interesting work. Our citizen army consists of all sorts and conditions of men and we come into contact with private soldiers in every station of life.

Only a week or two ago I was talking to a soldier returning to France after leave who was a lecturer in Decorative Art at Leeds University. Another day I came across a private of good social position from my last parish, and I have met our late postman from W. Winch.

Up to last week most of us chaplains lived in a boarding

PARISH MAGAZINE.
1918

house, but meals were so irregular that it interfered with our work and we were unable to get a chance of quiet for study. Now, four of us have taken upon ourselves the responsibility of house-keeping. We have taken a furnished house and draw our rations from the army. We are not quite settled down yet, but we feel quite comfortable, and are able to arrange matters to suit our work.

WOLFERTON

CONGRATULATIONS to Sergt. R. Curson, who has been awarded the Star of Mons, in addition to the Military Medal he received some time ago. Sergt. Lewis Curson is in hospital at Inverness, having been gassed, but we are glad to hear he is doing well.

CASTLE RISING & ROYDON

RECEIVED by Mrs. Cator, Castle Rising; -

Fairfield Hospital, Kent.

Dear Madam, - Just a few lines as perhaps you would like to know the history of one of your eggs, which I am glad to say I received at a General Hospital in France, and I thank you very much for the same. Well, friend, you will have to excuse me for not writing before, as I was unconscious for four days, and on coming round I had an appetite for an egg, and they gave me the lucky one. Being sent to England I lost your address, until I came across my belongings, and as I have now found it I thought I would write acknowledging it. I don't know whether this letter will find you or not, but I hope you and all at home and away are in good health. Hoping you will not be disappointed with me at taking such a liberty.

Believe me to be,

yours sincerely

(Cpl.) J. SANDHAM.

FOR the year ending March 30, 1918, 758 eggs have been sent for wounded soldiers, making a total of 3,745 during the past three years.

£1/2/0 was sent to the Church Army in Lent for Recreation Huts for the soldiers.

CASTLEACRE

The Sale organised for funds for the Hospital Supply Working Party's materials, was a great success. Most generous were the givers of all sorts of saleable things: from huge carrots down to hat pins! And most generous were those who came to buy. Over £14 was realised. A bale of flannelette now costs between £5 and £6, and this quality is soon exhausted in providing bandages for willing workers at the Depot to make. Last quarter, ending March 1st, 1388 items were sent off.

PARISH MAGAZINE.
1918

NARBOROUGH & NARFORD

MILITARY FUNERALS. - On Feb. 21st, the body of Sec. Lieutenant Charles Arkley Law, R.F.C. - 18 - and on Feb. 26th, the body of Sec. Lieutenant Harold Augustus Laws, R.F.C. - 23 - both of 26th Sq., were buried in our Churchyard. It is a startling commentary on the uncertainty of life and its tragedies, to note that Lieutenant Laws was in charge of the firing party at the burial of Lieutenant Law, only five days previous to his own burial. In both cases beautiful wreaths covered the coffins.

WOLFERTON

Pte. Ernest Hudson writing from Palestine on Feb. 2nd, says, "These last three weeks we have been road making among orange and lemon plantations. We can have an orange whenever we like, and it's nothing to see oranges as large as coconuts. It is a very pretty sight I can assure you, as the trees are laden, and the plantations are from three to four miles long. No doubt you have heard of Jaffa oranges. This is where they grow.

LITTLE MASSINGHAM

Pte. Richard Barnes has been severely wounded, and he is in a hospital in France.

Pte. F. Neale had a severe attack of fever in France, and is now convalescing at Totnes, in Devonshire.

___

A VERY successful concert in aid of the Norfolk Red Cross Society, arranged by Mrs. Dring and Miss McAnally, was held in the Parish Room on Wednesday, April 10th. £18 was realised, which, as the Secretary said, in acknowledging the money, it is the largest contribution from a village concert to the funds of the Society.

THE Little Massingham Depot has sent 1032 eggs for the wounded from the five villages - Great and Little Massingham, Harpley, Raynham and Weasenham during the first three months of the year.

NORTH RUNCTON

These are anxious days for all of us, more especially for those who have their loved ones at the Front, and to these we extend our utmost sympathy.

Up to the present I am thankful to say that, as far as we know, all those who are especially in our thoughts and prayers are safe. Further news of Stanley Chilvers is anxiously awaited, and I hope and trust we shall soon hear that his wounds are not serious. Meanwhile we must continue to watch and pray, and be content to leave all things to our Heavenly Father's will.

1918

LITTLE MASSINGHAM

ON April 28th, we had special collections for the Norfolk Prisoners of War. We were able to send to the Committee the good contributions of £4/6/1.

FRED. Callaby has recently left the Village to join a Labour Battalion. Our good wishes go with him; also with Fred Neale, who has come home from hospital on a short leave before returning to his regimental depot in Ireland.

NEWS has been received that Major (Temp. Lt. Col.) D. L. Brereton has been awarded the D.S.O. He is in command of a battalion which was very heavily engaged on the first day of the great offensive in France.

ANOTHER decoration, less directly connected with the parish, is that of Flight-Commander F. Williams recently a pupil at the Rectory. He has received the Croix de guerre, the highest French award for **bravery.**

ANMER

WE greatly regret that Mr. and Mrs. John Carter have lost another son - Albert, and this makes the third in this sad war. He was well known to all of us, and we had a Memorial Service after Evensong on Sunday, June 2nd. Mr. and Mrs. Carter, and other members of the family were present, including Private Herbert Carter, another

son who has been badly wounded. The chancel had been adorned with stately palms and other pot flowers, two laurel wreaths being placed on either side of the entrance and a large cross of laurel on the steps before the altar.

ASHWICKEN

MISSION ROOM BIBLE CLASS. - On Monday, 3rd June, 16 members had an outing to Hunstanton. Starting at 9.30 in carriages, we had a delightful drive through Sandringham, where the woods were looking their best with the Rhododendrons in full bloom. Arrived at Hunstanton, we dispersed to amuse ourselves on the beach, where paddling &c. was indulged in. At 4 o'clock we all assembled in Mrs. Cresswell's garden, where we enjoyed war tea. At 5.45 we packed ourselves into the carriages again and started on our homeward journey, getting back about 9 o'clock tired and sunburnt, but having thoroughly enjoyed our day out.

WAR NEWS. - We are glad to notice in the recent list of honours, the name of Captain Gerald Groom, has been awarded the Military Cross. He is now at the Front acting as Brigade Major.

GAYTON THORPE & EAST WALTON

WE are sorry to hear that Pte. John Curl, 2/5th Lincolnshire

1918

Regiment, of "Old Barn," Gayton Thorpe, who has been officially reported missing since 15th April last; we are thankful to hear that he is still alive, though a prisoner of war in German hands.

NEWS has been received that Acting Coy. Sergt. Major Philip Green, Royal Engineers, has been awarded the Military Medal - he is to be congratulated on winning this distinction.

FLITCHAM

WORK done by our Red Cross Working Party between March 12th and June 18th, and sent to Norwich War Hospital Supply Depot was - 550 roller bandages, 4 chest bandages, 44 abdominal bandages, 19 capelines, 10 bed jackets, 31 pairs bed socks, 10 snippet limb pillows, 30 pocket handkerchiefs, 12 flannel vests, 11 waste pads, 1 pair operation stockings, 10 wound pads, 4 slings; Total 736.

LITTLE MASSINGHAM

A NEW movement has been set on foot through the country to form Women's Institutes, designed in the first instance to meet the special needs of these times, but also to be permanent centres for the development of home and rural life, and to promote local industries, and also for educational advantages.

NORTH RUNCTON

We have to record the death of Joseph Steward, who died in France from the effects of gas poisoning. At one time his recovery was thought possible, but it was not to be.

SOUTH WOOTTON

A VERY sad accident happened on Whitsun Tuesday to Kathleen Toll, who was run over by a motor and killed instantly. The child was a regular attendant at our Day and Sunday Schools.

WEST WINCH

Dover,
22nd June 1918

My dear Friends, -

As long as the **war** lasts the loss of life, and the maiming of men **for** life, is appalling. God grant the end may be near. We realise the fact that we are at war most when any from our midst is missing or wounded.

Our daughter's husband after being in a French hospital for three weeks where he was unable to get a letter from home, arrived at a London hospital on the night of the 20th, and I was able to see him on my way back to Dover on the 21st. The officers in his regiment suffered heavily, and he thinks himself fortunate in coming through so well. He speaks highly of the French doctor who attended him. He is doing splendidly but I fear it will be some time before he is able to walk properly. He received a gunshot wound through the foot. We thank God he is back in England for a time rather than being in a French hospital and subject to German bomb-dropping.

I am yours faithfully,

W. T. GIFFORD.

WOLFERTON

HER Majesty Queen Alexandra, accompanied by Princess Victoria and attended by the Ladies-in-waiting, was present at Divine Service in our Church on Sunday evening, June 9th. The Rector officiated. There was a full choir and the singing was good.

THE school children have sent 3/6 to the Fund for Blind soldiers' children. The same amount to the Overseas Club for presents for the soldiers.

CASTLE RISING & ROYDON

CONGRATULATIONS.

Sergeant Major Harry Leggett, has been promoted to Staff Quarter Master Sergeant; Alfred Nurse and Edward Smith, have both been commended by their C.O. and Brigade Commander for having distinguished themselves by conspicuous bravery in the field.

During operations these soldiers galloped under heavy fire while the roads were kept under a continuous barrage and delivered an important message to advanced Headquarters. The safe delivery of this message resulted in the reserve section of the Battalion being in position at the time the enemy attacked a particular point.

JOHN Marsters, recently called to the colours and posted to the Grenadier Guards, has been suffering from measles and influenza. James Bocking, another of our splendid young soldiers, has been wounded in the knee. Both are happily making good progress towards recovery.

U.M.C.A. – A very interesting address was given by the Rev. W. Brooke, organizing secretary for the Eastern Counties, on behalf of the mission at the Reading Room on July 23rd. He gave instances, of the cruelty of German rule in East Africa, and demonstrated the crime it would be to betray those who have trusted us, by handing them over, after the war, to the hated German rule - this, for them, would mean torture, slavery and massacre.

FLITCHAM

VEGETABLE COLLECTION. - The School children, under the direction of the head mistress (Miss M. Jones) and her sister Miss G. Jones, are making a monthly collection of fruit, vegetables and eggs for the V.A.D. hospital at Norwich. These collections were commenced on May 30th, and the last Thursday in each month is the day fixed for this purpose. On June 27th every child contributed something, and their offerings were then sent to Miss Jarvis, Hillington, and by her despatched to Norwich.

GAYTON THORPE & EAST WALTON

SUNDAY, Aug. 4th, the day on which we enter the fifth year of the war is to be kept as a special Day of Intercession and Prayer, and it is hoped that everyone will do their utmost to attend the Services.

THE School was inspected in religious subjects on Thursday July 11th, by the Rev. J. B. Alexander. The report has just been received - it is not quite such a good report as last year.

EVERY one seems to have enjoyed the trip to Snettisham beach. The weather was fine on each occasion; it was rather cold on June 27th for those from E. Walton, but it was a lovely day on the following Thursday for Gayton Thorpe. A fine summer's day at the seaside is certainly one of the pleasures of this life.

LITTLE MASSINGHAM

THE Women's Institute was successfully inaugurated on July 17th. A meeting is to be held on the first Wednesday afternoon in each month, alternately at Little and Great Massingham, beginning Aug. 7th. The annual subscription is 2/-.

MRS. Burton has received a birthday cablegram from her son James from Cairo.

NORTH RUNCTON

My dear Friends,

We have entered upon another year of war, the first day of which was observed as a day of humble Intercession to Almighty God. At the time of writing the news is cheering, and makes one hope that the end is really in sight. Victory and peace will best come, however, not of our own choosing but of God's, and we must learn more and more our dependence upon Him, and as we continue faithfully to carry out the duties entrusted to us, we may be sure that He will answer our prayers.

GRIMSTON

ON Remembrance Day four years had passed since the day on which we entered the war, Aug 4th, 1914, a day forever great in the annals of our country. Since then Grimston has sent two hundred of its sons to aid the cause, and 26 have made the great sacrifice. All were remembered in our Remembrance Day services, and our offering which amounted to £4/12/6, were given to the Norfolk Branch of the British Red Cross Society.

PARISH MAGAZINE.
1918

WEST WINCH

Dover,
20th July, 1918.

My dear Friends, -

Today the war news is better than it has been for some time. May it continue good, but we must not be depressed if we get any set back. It may ebb and flow for sometime yet. We hope it won't, but we must be prepared for it may it be the beginning of the end. While we all feel war weary, we know it must go on till the enemy is beaten. A patched up peace would make another war inevitable very soon on a larger scale, if possible. The successful counter attack of the French and Americans on the 17th, gives us an idea of what is likely to be the result when the Americans enter the war in force. This year may not see the end, but it may give us some hope of a speedy finish.

If we believe we are fighting in the Cause of righteousness let us pray that the God of righteousness will guide our rulers, our soldiers and sailors, and help them to bring this war to a speedy and victorious end.

I am, yours faithfully,
W. T. GIFFORD.

———

Shoreham-by-Sea,
21st September, 1918.

My dear Friends, -

You will see from above address I have left Dover. I was ordered to report here on August 30th, so that now I have had three weeks of camp life. Here there is a large convalescent camp, which means this is a very healthy place. I have nothing to do with the convalescent camp. I am placed with the Artillery and my camp is about two miles from Shoreham. I have also the Flying Corps with another unit four miles away, so my work is somewhat varied.

The name of the place where our camp is situated is called "The Happy Valley." The name is no doubt very appropriate during summer and in peaceful times, but to be encamped in it during present weather conditions, well, the name doesn't suit it. I don't know what it will be like in winter if we cannot get any coal. Anyway our men in France are facing worse conditions, and as we think of them we feel it is our duty to meet the conditions of our life cheerfully. I am always thinking of our boys who are fighting so bravely and successfully. I am sorry to learn that Clifford Drew has been wounded, and R. J. Carter again for the fourth time. I am glad to know that Carter is getting on well, and is at present in a convalescent camp in France.

Let us pray for a speedy end to the war and safe return of our boys home.

I am, yours faithfully,
W. T. GIFFORD.

PARISH MAGAZINE.
1918

EDITORIAL - PAPER COST

THE cost of paper having advanced over 400 percent above the pre-war level, the Magazine can no longer be produced for 1d per copy. The cost to the different parishes varies from upwards of 2½d to 1½d each. Depending on the length of copy sent by each parish.

LITTLE MASSINGHAM

HARVEST has begun under the most, favourable weather conditions. Reports from most parts of the country speak of a very bountiful harvest. In this parish there is a Harvest Camp of 26 boys from the North Eastern County School, Barnard Castle, under the command of Capt. R J. Bunting, assisted by Lieut. Ord. The boys, who have come a long way and given up a big slice of their holidays, are at work on farms in Great and Little Massingham and Harpley.

NORTH RUNCTON

We are being warned by those who are in a position to know that we must expect to suffer hardship this coming winter owing to the difficulty in procuring coal. Let us brace ourselves to bear bravely and cheerfully whatever trials we may have to undergo. We have a great deal to be thankful for, and compared with those in other countries such as Belgium, France and Italy, we have not felt the real pinch of war. It may be our turn to share more acutely the sufferings and privations of others. Acting on the best advice, I have decided to suspend the Coal Club for the time being - I much regret having to do so and hope the members will not be seriously inconvenienced.

ASHWICKEN

SCHOOL NEWS. - Our children have collected during the month of July and August, 58 eggs, which have been forwarded by Miss Norah Groom to the convalescent home established at Hillington Hall for wounded officers.

HILLINGTON

THE Hillington Patriotic Fund is subscribing twelve shillings a month to the parcels which are being sent to Pte. Elijah Simmons, who is a prisoner of war in Germany.

LITTLE MASSINGHAM

26 lbs of sheep's wool, collected by the school children of Great and Little Massingham, Ashwicken and Castle Rising, have been sent to the London Depot.

NORTH RUNCTON

My dear Friends,

A public meeting will be held shortly at which you will be invited to help to win the war by

PARISH MAGAZINE.
1918

buying war Bonds. This is being done by many of the surrounding villages; Setch has already made a start, and I hope North Runcton and West Winch will soon fall into line. Mr. Gurney, who represents North Runcton, will explain fully how to set about buying these bonds, though I have no doubt that most of you know something about the working of the scheme.

WOLFERTON

Apologies if some of the content below offends. The article has been reprinted exactly as it was originally written. It would not be correct to rewrite historical material. Ed.

MR. Hodges' brother, who is serving with His Majesty's forces in Africa, writes on June 28th: -

"Several interesting events have happened during the last week or two, among them being the capture of a young Zebra, which we are now keeping in camp.

Also, last week a huge hippopotamus was shot at the lake close by. It was a massive beast, and a bullock waggon had to be utilized to get it back to the camp. The thickness of the hide is surprising, and after it had been skinned it took about ten niggers to move the hide, and even then they could not lift it off the ground. The hide is used for whips, switches, and even walking sticks after it has been cut into the required strips and dried in the sun."

CASTLE RISING & ROYDON

A WAR Savings Association has recently started for Castle Rising. Rather late in the day, better late than never, especially at this critical time, when a great spurt is needed to bring the war to a successful conclusion.

WOLFERTON

WE regret to hear that Mr. Hazel's brother, who had been wounded in the head, has lost the sight of both eyes. A friend of his (who has also lost the sight of one eye) writing from hospital, says: - "I am more than sorry to say he has lost the greatest thing that, God ever gave to man, his sight."

FLIGHT Sergt. A. Jex, who was reported missing, is a prisoner of war in Germany, and this information has, no doubt, given great relief to his anxious parents.

ASHWICKEN

During the month of October 240 lbs. of blackberries have been gathered by the children. They have been despatched to the Divisional Agent for the purpose of Jam making.

WEST WINCH

West Winch Rectory,

21st October 1918, -

My dear Friends,

I am just home for five days leave, which will possibly be my last leave before returning home for good. Last Friday I left Shoreham – by – Sea bound for Colchester, and so have another change of work to return to. The war news keeps very good, and many people think it will soon be over.

I am, yours faithfully,

W. T. GIFFORD

NARBOROUGH & NARFORD

OUR BOYS. - At Narborough we have all been saddened at the death, after a severe operation carried out at the Front, of Albert Turner. Mrs. Turner has had two kindly worded letters from the chaplain, who was with her husband in his last hours. Albert Turner was much esteemed at Swaffham and in the neighbouring villages.

To all this sad news we have to add that of William Powley's death. He had only been three weeks in France. Wounded and gassed on Nov. 7th, he was laid to rest on the following day. Deep sympathy goes out to his young wife and his parents. Had he lived till Nov. 12th, he would have been 26.

The younger Bolman has landed in Mesopotamia in good spirits, and W. Turner has got his sergeant's stripes. He too is in Mesopotamia and appears to be flourishing.

Sergeant Albert Pitcher is at a N.C.O. School in York, preparing for special duties.

Edward Powley, R.N. - a B.A. of London University - has been ordered to China for some special work.

Mr. and Mrs. Dupuis recently visited us: Mr. Dupuis has been at the Front in R.F.A., engaged in the dangerous duty of bringing up ammunition, literally in "feeding the guns." It may be added that Mr. Dupuis has purchased property near Brandon.

In the midst of rejoicings we mourn deeply our losses. Narford records the death on Nov. 3, in France, of Henry Reynolds. Irreparable as is his widow's loss, it will be softened by the knowledge of how greatly her husband was esteemed when at the Red Lodge.

CASTLE RISING & ROYDON

SINCE October 20th when our last notes were written, momentous events have happened with startling rapidity.

Turkey, Austria, Hungary and Germany surrendered between

1918

October 30th and November 11th. The terms of the armistice made between these countries and the allies were so drastic, that no further fighting can be possible. Thus all we have been fighting for has been attained, and the judgement of God has been made so visible, that it is apparent to all men. The next step is the Peace Conference and reconstruction.

As we applied ourselves wholeheartedly to the business of the war, we must in like manner apply ourselves to the business of building up the new world. There was a spontaneous outburst of thanksgiving to Almighty God throughout the country.

WEST WINCH

Colchester,

21st Nov, 1918.

My dear Friends, -

When we received news of the signing of the armistice we were all filled with joy because we knew the fighting and loss of life was practically over. Great as our joy was it was mingled with tears. In the letter I sent to be read on the day of Thanksgiving, Nov. 17th, I expressed the hope that a Memorial should be placed in the Church in memory of the boys from our parish who had given up their lives for us.

On that day I think we all felt that God had given us the victory and we must thank Him for it. The 700 soldiers at my service were most reverent and fervent. I trust our spirit of thankfulness is not a temporary effervescence, but lasting, and that we shall show it in the reconstruction which is to take place in the country. If the Country is to be built up on new foundations we need men of sanctified common sense to lay those foundations.

We are told there will be a new England after the war. God grant it may be a better, nobler and purer England, that is built on righteousness, where all shall receive what is justly due, with employers and the work people dealing honestly with each other and seeking each other's good.

There seems to me a danger of selfish interest causing us to loose our heads and thus ruining our country. I trust the example of Russia will prevent this. There are people who put self and party interests before the good of the country. I have faith in the general common sense and level headedness of the majority of the people of our country and so I look hopefully to the future.

Best wishes for Christmas.

I am,
yours faithfully,

W. T. GIFFORD.

NORTH RUNCTON

The news of the signing of the armistice has brought us all great joy and thankfulness, of which our thanksgiving services bore full witness. We have had to sorrow over the loss of six or seven who went from this village, but one cannot help feeling most thankful to Almighty God that so many have been spared. Now we look for their home-coming, though we may have to wait a little while, but when they do come, I am Sure we shall make it worthy of them.

NORTH PICKENHAM, WITH HOUGHTON-ON-THE-HILL.

In our little village we have special reasons for rejoicing at the signing of the armistice - because the total number of names on our "Roll of Honour" is well over sixty - that is more than one-fifth of our population. How glad and how thankful we shall be to see them back again! I hope we shall never forget what they have done for us. And how we shall miss those who will not return. They will be always in our remembrance: and the supreme sacrifice, which they have been called upon to make, has not been in vain.

We are grateful to the Rev. Thorp for allowing the use of the last quote.

The presentation of this page is intended to show our respect to those who died or suffered and to the many who fought and survived. Ed.

PARISH MAGAZINE.
1919

LITTLE MASSINGHAM

IT may be of interest to record that our **War** Savings Association in this parish is now 2½ years' old, has a membership of 70, and has invested £625. The certificates when they mature in five years from date of purchase will be worth over £800. If held under the new scheme for ten years, their joint value will run into four figures.

WEST WINCH

Colchester,

21st Dec. 1918.

My dear Friends,-

When you get this letter Christmas will be past, the first for four years without any fighting, and I hope it has been a happy and blessed time for you all. And now at the beginning of a New Year may I wish you a very bright, happy and peaceful New Year. We have passed through four years of anxiety such as I hope we shall never experience again. The last two months have been full of excitement. First the Armistice filled us with thankfulness to God for the signs of peace, then came the election, the results of which are not known at the time of writing. As the future happiness and prosperity of our country greatly depends upon the kind of men we send to represent us in parliament, it is to be hoped the people have elected men who mean business, and not men full of fads and self-seeking.

The problem of reconstruction will require the best brains of the country if it is to be successfully done. I hope men competent to do the work will have been elected.

It will perhaps be some time before all our boys get home. The army is now being gradually demobilised, but peace terms have not yet been settled. It will depend on those terms when the armies will be fully dispersed and our boys return home.

I am hoping to return home about Jan. 27th and begin our regular services on the first Sunday of February.

I am, yours faithfully,

W. T. GIFFORD

HILLINGTON

We cannot regret the death of Mrs. Curson. She died just when to live would have been a burden to her, but we shall most of us miss her.

NORTH RUNCTON

Sunday School Christmas Treat was held on Saturday, Dec. 28th. Mrs. Digby gave each child a present. These Mrs. Gurney distributed, after which came a lantern display of slides supplied by the Royal Society for the

PARISH MAGAZINE.

1919

Prevention of Cruelty to Animals. Mr Alexander kindly brought his lantern. The rest of the time was spent in games.

WEST WINCH

Colchester.

21st Jan., 1919.

My dear Friends, -

I am disappointed. I hoped to be among you before this magazine was issued, but now I fear it is not possible. About the middle of December I sent in the usual notice to resign my chaplaincy. The notice was returned with the message that by an order issued early in December the application for my demobilisation must be made by my Bishop to the Archbishop of Canterbury. I at once wrote to ask the Bishop of Norwich to apply for my release, and by return had a post card from him saying he had placed my name on the Archbishop's list.

So far I have had no notice of my release, and whether it may come soon or late I have not the least idea. I am informed it is possible the town clergy will be sent home first. If so, I shall have to stay for a time, unless the Bishop presses for my release, which I hope he will. After two years' absence I feel I ought to be back. Expecting to be back at the end of January, I did not take the 12 days Christmas leave given to all soldiers serving at home during December and the beginning of January. I hope I may have the good fortune soon to return home. In the meantime Mr. Plumptre has promised to carry on.

I am, yours faithfully,

W. T. GIFFORD.

WOLFERTON

QUITE a gloom was cast over the village on Sunday morning, Jan. 19th, when it became known that Prince John had passed away on the previous evening.

The late Prince's residence amongst us will always revive happy memories, and he will be missed most of all by the school children.

ASHWICKEN

VILLAGE CONCERT. - A most successful concert was held in our Mission Room on Wednesday evening Feb. 12th, for the purpose of paying off the debt incurred in consequence of the Room being thoroughly cleaned, whitewashed and coloured. Every available seat was occupied, and our hearty thanks are due to Mr. and Mrs. Boam for arranging such a pleasant evening's entertainment.

FLITCHAM

H.M. The Queen, accompanied by H.R.H. Princess Mary, visited the School on January 28th and distributed her annual gifts to the teachers and children. The recipients were greatly pleased with the gifts and by Her Majesty's gracious words.

LITTLE MASSINGHAM

We regret to record a sad accident to Bertie Gibson, who was run over by a cart and had to be taken to the Lynn Hospital. We hope he will soon be completely cured.

WEST WINCH

Colchester

21st Feb. 1919.

My dear Friends,

Before this letter was due for the press I hoped to hear definitely when I should be released. The Bishop has asked for my speedy release. And I know I shall be among the first demobilised. I am still hoping I may get home before the magazine comes into your hands.

I am, yours faithfully,

W. T. GIFFORD

WOLFERTON

On Friday Feb. 7th, H.M. The King visited the school for the purpose of presenting Geoffrey Haverly with a handsome Bible as a prize for Religious Knowledge. The inscription inside was in His Majesty's own handwriting.

FLITCHAM

COAL AND CLOTHING CLUB. - Forty-five members paid in between May and October £39/16/4. To this sum a bonus (towards which H.M. The King subscribes yearly £2/2/0) of 1d. in the shilling was added. Those members who chose clothing were able to be supplied, but, through the great difficulty of procuring coal, those who desired coal could not be supplied and were therefore repaid their money with the bonus added.

NORTH WOOTTON

HOSPITAL BAGS. - This fund is now closed. 1480 bags have been made and sent from this parish, and there is a balance in hand of £4/2/0, which will be handed over to the fund which will in all probability endow a bed in a hospital.

HILLINGTON

We think everyone knows that a Flitcham and Hillington Institute for Women has been started at the Rifle Range, Flitcham, and Lady ffolkes is President. Membership, 2/- yearly. The object is to bring women together socially and for the purpose of instruction and amusement. We believe that only one from Hillington has joined as a member. It is hoped that Hillington means to give the movement a trial, other places in Norfolk are already making it a big success.

WEST WINCH

West Winch Rectory,

21st March 1919.

My dear Friends,-

After just over two years' absence from the parish I have at last been demobilised, and returned home on the 11th. I am glad to get back to my work here, although while the war was going on I felt there was a greater sphere of usefulness for me with the army, and if I could be of any use to the dear boys who were fighting for us it was my duty to be with them to give such counsel, help, encouragement and comfort, as I could.

I am, yours faithfully,

W. T. GIFFORD

Photos on page 95

LITTLE MASSINGHAM

The arrangements for the coming peace celebration were discussed at a Parish Meeting on May 17th. It was agreed to have sports, cricket with fancy dress competition, a light tea, a more substantial supper, followed by a short Thanksgiving Service in Church. The day is to close with a bonfire, flares and rockets.

NORTH RUNCTON

The decision come to at the meeting recently held to erect a Tablet in Church and a Cross in the Village, to perpetuate the memory of those who laid down their lives in the Great War will, I feel sure, meet with everyone's approval. Both the Church and the Village will thus have something to revere and cherish for future generations.

CASTLE RISING & ROYDON

AT a Committee meeting of the Castle Rising War Memorial held on Thursday, June 12th, it was finally decided that the memorial should take three forms, viz:-

1. Two standard lamps to be erected at the cross roads in the centre of the Parish.

2. A mural tablet to be placed in the Church, to the Glory of God and in memory of the men of the parish who made the supreme sacrifice, with their names inscribed.

3. A book with the names of all those men of the Parish of Castle Rising who served in the war.

Subscriptions to the above are invited. A list of subscribers is to be placed at the Post Office and on the Church door, and subscriptions are to be paid to Col. C. A. Howard, Treasurer.

PARISH MAGAZINE.
1919

GRIMSTON

No greater month has ever passed in our day and generation. The Treaty of Peace was signed on Saturday, June 28th, and the news was received in Grimston in the early evening. Everywhere there was great rejoicing. The bells pealed out their loudest, and soon a congregation had gathered in the Parish Church and with full hearts joined in hymns and psalms and thanksgivings.

NORTH WOOTTON

THANKSGIVING FOR PEACE
On Sunday July 6th, the day appointed by Royal Proclamation for thanksgiving for the conclusion of Peace, our Services were well attended, and real gratitude was apparent amongst us for the good hand of Almighty God in bringing the war to such a happy end.

SOUTH WOOTTON

A meeting of the War Memorial Committee, to which all of the parishioners were invited to attend, was held to decide the form the War Memorial should take. It was unanimously decided that a monument some thirteen feet high with a plain cross on the top should be erected in the Churchyard, so placed so that all those who pass by may see it. The names of the fallen will be engraved on the monument.

EDITORIAL.

Owing to the Railway Strike and other unavoidable causes, the Magazines for Oct. did not reach several of the parishes until the 21st. Under these exceptional circumstances subscribers will understand that it was impossible to post the magazines sooner.

NORTH RUNCTON

Let us hope and pray that this peace which has been won at such a sacrifice may not be disturbed by industrial strife and unrest.

WEST WINCH

I received a letter from the Bishop asking if I could arrange a visit to the West Winch Oil Works. Permission was readily given for his lordship to see the works and Col. Seppings very kindly lent his car to bring him from and to the station. Mr Frazer the chief chemist, explained the process of extracting oil from the shale, the gases which were produced, and the various by-products which would be valuable for aniline dyes, as well as for many other important uses.

Photo on page 96

CONGHAM

Two of our school-girls, Frances Bullen and Ivy Watts, have made a house-to-house collection for the Prevention of Cruelty to Children. £2 was raised.

A Unique Photograph

When Rosemary, co-producer of this book acquired the old parish magazines, she also found this picture in a tortoiseshell frame. It was of the Rev. Alwyne Rice R.N. (Rector of Wolferton) who married Cicely Brereton, Rosemary's great aunt. Obviously this picture and frame was treasured by the Rev. Rice because of the number of enlarged prints of this photograph found close by.

Written on the back
of the photo:

"Photograph taken
by Queen Alexandra
herself and given to
me in this frame
Xmas 1919"

It was known that Queen Alexandra and Queen Mary and other members of the Royal Family were visitors to the Wolferton Rectory and the Rev. Rice also paid regular visits to Prince John who was living close by. Ed.

PARISH MAGAZINE.
1920

NORTH WOOTTON

THE HEATING APPARATUS. At the time of the printing of the Magazines, the new Church heating is being tested with every prospect of its proving an entire success.

SOUTH WOOTTON

SOUTH WOOTTON RECTORY, 21st January 1920.

My very dear Friends,

I thank you from the bottom of my heart for all the sympathy and kindness you have given me in my sorrow since I arrived on 3rd January.

I have been trying to persuade my father to come and live with us, as we could tell he was failing, but he could not bear the thought of leaving South Wootton and all his friends; some of whom were here when he and mother came to live here in May, 1882. 38 years is a long time to be in one Parish, and at late years father was unable to do all that he would have liked to do for you, but I am sure you will make allowances for him. As far as we know, no appointment has yet been made, but may I express the hope that when your new Rector comes, you will make him feel that South Wootton is his home in the fullest sense of the word.

Good-bye, my friends, and God bless you. HILDA M. BAKER.

ASHWICKEN

The County Assistant Medical Inspector visited our school on Friday, 7th May, the result of which was that he selected 15 cases which needed treatment. On the other hand he considered that the state of the children's teeth was on the whole exceptionally good.

LITTLE MASSINGHAM

The Memorial Panelling in the Chancel is completed, a beautiful piece of work, by Messrs. Cornish and Gaymer. The dedication will take place on a date in July to be announced. It was hoped that the War Memorial Tablet would be ready for the same occasion, but Messrs. Powell have been delayed by the large number of Memorials entrusted to them.

WEST WINCH

I regret the Magazines were so late in delivery last month, the fault was with the carrier. They were handed to him on 1st June and remained in the carrier's van until 19th June, when the printer got them from him and brought them. I hope in future they will not be delayed through the carelessness of the carrier.

NORTH RUNCTON

Our War Memorial is, I am sorry to say, a long time making its appearance. There has been some

PARISH MAGAZINE.
1920 - 1921

difficulty in procuring the stone of which it is to be made. Our best thanks are due to those who so kindly went round collecting money for it. There are still some houses to be visited and so far a very satisfactory response has been made to the appeal.

HILLINGTON

Following a special collection, £2/5/1 was sent to the Colchester Idiot Asylumn.

LITTLE MASSINGHAM

The Service of Dedication of the Oak Panelling in the Chancel in Memory of the late Rector was held at 6 o'clock on Monday, 19th July. The Church was filled for the occasion. Boy Scouts and Girl Guides lined the path by which the Clergy entered.

NORTH RUNCTON

Mrs. Digby left in her will to the Rector and Churchwardens for the time being £100 to be invested, the annual income to be applied towards the expenses of keeping the paths in the Churchyard and the grass cut and generally towards keeping the Churchyard in good order and condition. A cheque for £100 has already been received which will be suitably invested in order to carry out her wishes in a matter which, as everyone knows, was very dear to her heart. Her kind act will be appreciated by all.

FLITCHAM

The War Memorial at Sandringham was unveiled and dedicated by H.M. The King on Sunday afternoon 17th October. Hundreds of people attended from all the villages round. The Memorial is to the memory of the men on the Sandringham Estate who fell in the war. On it are chiselled the names of the fallen, seventy-seven in number, in alphabetical order, including twenty-one from the parish of Flitcham. The Memorial, which is a very beautiful Cross, stands close to the public entrance to Sandringham Park.

1921

WEST WINCH

The year 1920 has been one of trouble and unrest, what is 1921 to be? We hope it will bring to us a state of stability and rest. At present all seems dark and uncertain with trade unstable, lack of employment, high prices, &c., increasing rates and heavy taxation, the immediate future seems gloomy. We are told this has always been the case after a great war, and it takes some time before the Country can get back to settled conditions, let us not be despondent but hopefully look forward to the New Year bringing a more settled and restful state in our country. But do not let us forget that if this desired result is

PARISH MAGAZINE.
1921

to be brought about we must do all we can to get rid of the spirit of materialism and selfishness which has taken possession of the nation. Until the Spirit of Christ governs all classes Society and our Politicians, we can not be assured of any lasting peace. Let us not only pray for rest and peace, but let us work for it by giving ourselves heartily to the service of Christ and trying to lead others to Him.

I am afraid I cannot say much that is cheering or encouraging concerning the spiritual growth of the Parish during the past year. Since the war our congregations have been of a very fluctuating character. A spirit of indifference appears to have come over us, and I trust it will disappear with the old year.

Let us begin the New Year by working together heartily with mind, heart and soul for the Master. Whether the New Year is to be bright and happy or not depends largely upon ourselves. Shall we do our best to make it so?

With all good wishes for a Bright, Happy and Prosperous New Year to all.

NORTH RUNCTON

Our Lord's Temptation in the wilderness in which He had strength to have victory and to triumph over the world, the flesh, and the devil and for which conflict He found it needful to put Himself under severe discipline, should remind us that we too must practice some form of self-denial if we wish to gain His victory.

May I suggest something for everybody this Lent, which is a more rigid use of the means of grace? To Communicants, more frequent Communions. To Non-Communicants, more frequent attendance at Church, not only morning or evening but both, morning and evening where it is possible.

It will mean for some, getting up earlier than usual on Sunday morning, a sacrifice of one's own inclinations but for all who are in earnest about their spiritual welfare it will mean an influx of strength, a feeling that victory is in the air. So we shall find that we are more than conquerors through Him who loved us and gave Himself for us, and we shall be helping God to hasten His Kingdom.

HILLINGTON

A 'Flying Column' of Church Army Captains and Cadets, ten in number, is to make a pilgrimage from Birmingham to Yarmouth. The journey will take forty days and the men will stay for one night in a corresponding number of towns or villages. One of the stopping places is to be our own parish. We expect the men on 4th July, when they intend to hold evangelistic meetings at various suitable points. We shall be very grateful of any hospitality or assistance in providing for the comfort of the men.

NORTH RUNCTON

I am writing this from a sick room and I can only say how sorry I am that I should have been laid low at a time when I ought to have been up and doing things. But it can't be helped and I hope I shall soon be better and able to make up for lost time.

CASTLE RISING & ROYDON

PRONVILLE. - This Village was destroyed by the Germans. It consisted of 150 houses and is now being rebuilt by the inhabitants, who are returning to what was once their home. They are living in temporary shelters, doing all they can to clear up the wreckage and make a fresh start, but they require help in the shape of agricultural instruments and household utensils, etc. Lynn and North West Norfolk have adopted Pronville as their place to assist. It is the place where the 9th Batt. Norfolk Regiment distinguished themselves on 21st March, 1918.

The distress in this Country has been brought upon us by ourselves. Had it not been for the repeated strikes and unrest we might have been in a very different position to what we are today. The distress in France is the result of the German invasion.

It is proposed to have a stall in aid of Pronville at the Nursing Association rummage sale, to be held at the Rectory on Thursday, 14th July, at 3 p.m., and people are invited kindly to send to Mrs. Thursby what they are moved in their hearts to give to help their distressed friends in France with whom we fought side by side in the Great War.

LITTLE MASSINGHAM

The long drought, which is proving most serious for the fields and gardens, has favoured cricket. Both elevens have several victories to their credit.

NORTH RUNCTON

I am sorry that owing to my present state of health I have to take things as easily as possible. "Plenty of fresh air" the doctor says, and therefore I have not been going in and out of houses more than I have felt obliged. I have very reluctantly had to give up my School Inspection in religious knowledge for this year and I am sorry to say that no one has been found to take my place. I hope I shall soon get quite well again. The Sunday services will be as usual. Miss Nisbet, as you all know, is leaving us to be married after 18 years of faithful service in our School, and it goes without saying that she will be very greatly missed both by all the children and her friends. We only wish that Blackpool was not quite so far off.

___

The estimate for re-newing the Church Spire is so large that all thought of anything being done for the present is out of the question. All that can be done is to take it down to prevent its being any longer a source of danger to passers by and to hope that the Church Fabric account will soon be able to bear the expense of a new one.

WEST WINCH

The continued hot weather has brought the harvest upon us very quickly, once again to remind us of the sureness of God's promise "While the earth remaineth seed-time and harvest, and cold and heat, and night and day shall not cease." It reminds us too of the wisdom of living worthily and striving to produce such fruits of good living.

NORTH RUNCTON

I am hoping during this Winter to be able to invite any boys who like to come to the Rectory from 6 to 7 one evening in the week. Also I hope to arrange a Bible Study class for women and girls at the Rectory from 3 to 4.

I sincerely trust that those who are at present unemployed will soon be able to find work and that the outlook will brighten before winter really sets in.

___

GAYTON THORPE & EAST WALTON

I am requested to say that should the Nurse be required at any time, Mrs. Knight very kindly will allow a message to be sent by telephone to the Abbey at Westacre.

___

NORTH WOOTTON

The Men's Club and the Social Club are now in full swing again and they have the good wishes of all for a happy and successful season. An effort is being made to raise money to purchase a piano for the use of both Clubs and it is hoped that before long the required amount will be in hand.

WOLFERTON

The Boy Scouts are making good progress under Assistant Scoutmaster D. Batterbee, but the boys must remember that unless there is good discipline and perfect obedience the Boy Scouts movement will fail.

HILLINGTON

On Armistice Day the signal for observing the 2 minutes silence, of reverent memory of those who gave their lives in the Great War, was signalled by tolling of the Church Bell. It was hoped there would be a sale of the symbolic poppy Armistice Day, but though money was sent for the purchase of poppies in what seemed ample time the stock at headquarters was already exhausted.

1922

APOLOGY FROM THE PRINTER.

Owing to the length of the Christmas Holidays, and an unfortunate breakdown of my gas engine, the Magazines this month are much delayed. I trust my Clerical friends will bear with me under these circumstances, and every endeavour will be made in the future to ensure the Magazines being delivered in good time.

Every good wish for the New Year.

GEO. R. OSWELL.

CASTLE RISING & ROYDON

The collection on Christmas day for and "Waifs and Strays" amounted to 10/-, and that the Carol Service for St. Dunstan's Home for The Blind made 10/6. The Church was decorated with painstaking care, and those who gave their time to the work deserve our sincere thanks.

GRIMSTON

The year just ended has been one of great trial and anxiety. It has been described as the most disastrous year experienced in time of peace by this generation. But those best able to judge, unite in looking forward to the future in hopefulness. In the great matters which mean so much there is real cause for encouragement, and we trust therefore that the New Year will bring with it the better times we all desire.

NORTH RUNCTON

I wish you all a very happy and prosperous New Year. We still live in anxious times but let us hope that the world is slowly recovering, what we want to avoid is a relapse. The walls of the Temple of Peace are growing higher but there are enemies on all sides who try every endeavour to spoil and stop the building of it. Let us pray that the blessing of Almighty God may rest upon the labours of those who bear rule both in Church and State.

WEST WINCH

As a nation we have been passing through a period of gloom, unrest and anxiety and long for a time of restful progress, prosperity and happiness. Shall we all seek the help of Almighty God in the New Year and look forward hopefully to its bringing peace happiness and prosperity? With best wishes for a very happy and prosperous New Year to you all.

92

CONGHAM

CHRISTMAS TREE

Mr. and Mrs. Robert Elwes' splendid Christmas Treat was greatly appreciated by everyone. It was good to see 250 children looking so intensely happy when the Christmas Tree was stripped of its beautiful presents. Both Mr. and Mrs. Robert Elwes were untiring in their efforts to provide pleasure for so many children.

NORTH RUNCTON

It may interest you to know that according to a scheme set on foot by the Dean of Norwich, our parish will be specially remembered before God at the daily Celebration and weekly Intercessions in Norwich Cathedral.

Photo on page 96

WOLFERTON

On Tuesday, 17th January, the Queen, accompanied by Princess Mary, visited the school and gave presents to children and teachers, and on Friday, 20th Jan., Queen Alexandra who was accompanied by Princess Victoria, visited the school and gave presents to all.

ASHWICKEN

TRINITY HOSPITAL. - The Governess and Sisters gave the Princess Mary, as a wedding present, a Leather Blotter embossed with her initials in gold with a coronet above. The Governess attended the party given by the King and Queen at Buckingham Palace on 21st February.

LITTLE MASSINGHAM

The Church Army Van has spent a fortnight in Great Massingham where the Lantern and Mission services were well attended. Several from this Parish were able to go.

Photo on page 96

FLITCHAM

On Friday, 3rd March, H.M. The King, entertained all of the inhabitants of Flitcham and Harpley Dams. About 280 sat down to a substantial tea at 5.30, in a large barn, at the Abbey lent for occasion by Col. J. V. Betts. During the evening a telegram was sent by those present to H.M. The King, thanking him and respectfully offering their hearty congratulations to the Royal Bride and Bridegroom.

ASHWICKEN

There was only one application for the post of Head Mistress, it was from Miss Miles, and as her testimonials were considered most satisfactory she was elected unanimously; her duties are to commence in July next.

NORTH WOOTTON

The Choir at the present time is very weak in ladies' voices. The Rector would be very glad of offers of service from any ladies who are willing to help the worship of the Church in this way.

CASTLE RISING & ROYDON

We offer our sincere condolences with the relatives of Mrs. Edward Smith. She was a victim to the after-effects of influenza, which produced an affliction of peculiar painfulness and distress; this she endured with Christian resignation for a number of weeks, at length it pleased God to take her into that state where "the weary are at rest." Great sympathy is expressed for those who will miss her most. R.I.P.

LITTLE MASSINGHAM

SUNDAY SCHOOL TREAT. – A party of almost 40 mothers and children of the Sunday School spent an enjoyable afternoon at Sandringham and Wolferton on 19th July. The journey was made in Mr. R. E. Wilson's lorry. The Rector of Wolferton escorted the party at Sandringham, and with Mrs. Rice welcomed them at Wolferton Rectory.

Correction. - The expenses in connection with the Church Missionary Budget for the year were not £12 (as printed) but twelve shillings.

Sometimes it is very difficult to correct mistakes! Ed.

HILLINGTON

Holy Baptism 3rd Sept. Cythia, daughter of James Ernest and Sinly Twite.

HILLINGTON

The Printer made a mistake last month when notifying Mrs. Twile's name as Sinly, it was very plainly written as "Sinfy".

So was she Twile or Twite? Ed.

GRIMSTON

The committee would welcome additional subscribers to our Lending Library, which is now commencing its fourth year, with a new stock of sixty books. These will be changed at the end of the half-year for an entirely new set. Books can he obtained between 3 and 4 on Fridays. The charge for one volume, changed weekly if desired, is 3/- for six months, or one volume for one week, 2d. We have to thank Mrs. Hammond for kindly giving us seven volumes.

West Winch
Church
c1838

(David Apps)

The former
Rectory at
West Winch
c1838

(David Apps)

West Winch
National School
now the Church
Hall c1838

(David Apps)

Church Army Van outside West Winch Church (Date unknown)

North Runcton Church (Date unknown)

Before being converted to a bungalow, (now demolished) buildings similar to this were used for workshops and accommodation on the site of the English Oil Works at Setchey. Oil was extracted from the shale that came from the nearby quarry at West Winch. The works closed when the operation was no longer commercially viable.

The Hogge & Seppings Brewery at Setchey (Setch).
The business operated until 1928 when it was taken over by Bullards of Norwich. Bottom picture shows Brewery Cottages.

(David Apps)

(David Apps)

(David Apps)

Photos c1920

HILLINGTON

Owing to a new lighting installation, after much expense had been incurred in trying to get the old installation into working order, expenses connected with the organ and the usual running expenses of the Church and services, the Church funds were not in a position to pay the debts incurred. Mrs. Brereton most kindly came forward with an offer of help by organising a weekly entertainment. She arranged a most successful Whist Drive on the 27th October, which realised the most helpful sum of £2/12/0 for the funds. At the Whist Drive it was announced that Sir Everard ffolkes had most generously given £50 towards the payment of lighting installation. This news was received with acclamation.

The tolling of the Church Bell reminded all on Armistice Day to observe the two minutes silence, in memory of those who gave their lives in the Great War. It was a great pity that the police found it their duty to stop the sale of poppies by Hillington school children on 11th November. The sale was properly organized and controlled, and ten children wisely chosen to sell the poppies. A little judgement in such a case would further the help so pressingly needed for the ex-service men's funds. Fortunately the remaining store of poppies were disposed of privately.

CONGHAM

THINGS OLD. THE WILL OF HENRY SYMPSON, 1504.

I, Henry Sympson, Clerk and Rector of the Church of Congham St. Andrew, being of sound mind and good memory, make my testament &c &c. I leave and commend my soul to God Almighty, the Blessed Virgin Mary and all the Saints, and my body to be buried in the Chancel of the said Church before the High Altar there. I leave to the Gild of Holy Trinty *6/8,* to the Gild of St. John the Baptist *6/8.* I leave for a cope for the said Church 4 marks. I leave to the High Altar of Grymston *3/4,* to of the Gild of Corpus Christi there *2/0,* to the fabric of Grymston Church *6/8,* to the Guild of St. Botolph of Grymston *3/4* to the light of the Blessed Virgin Mary 20d. I leave to each Godson 12d. to the Fabric of the Church of the Blessed Mary of Congham *6/8,* to Margaret Nothyng 12d, to Thomas Sympson, Chaplain, my long gown of violet colour with a hood, to Henry Legate 4 silver spoons, if my creditors shall pay my executors the money &c., due to me All tithes and Autumn profits &c., of my said Church to be disposed by executors according to the constitutions of the Synod at Norwich by Walter Suffield, Bishop. All residue of goods not bequeathed I place at the disposition of my executors whom I appoint John Goole, Chaplain, to dispose for my soul's good and to the most pleasure of God.

Dated 5th March, 1503 (1504 our style). Proved 21st June 1504.

PARISH MAGAZINE.
1923

APOLOGIA.

The Printers very much regret being late in publishing the current number of the Parish Magazine. This is due to an unfortunate accident that occurred at the works at the time the Magazine was going to press. A very big beam that supported the roof collapsed bringing down with it a large portion of the ceiling, which caused general disorder, and meant holding up a great amount of work for several days. The machine on which the Magazine is printed being quite close to the disaster was unable to be worked until all the repairs were finished and everything cleared up.

ASHWICKEN

A Parish Gift. – The sons and daughters of the late Mrs. Howse have kindly presented our Parish with a bath chair, for which we offer grateful thanks. We shall miss our friends from Swiss Cottage, who have gone to live in Gayton.

LITTLE MASSINGHAM

The scheme to provide a District Nurse is slowly maturing. The annual cost will be a heavy one, but several subscriptions have come in. A nurse is not yet available, but it is expected that one will be appointed before the winter is over. Then we hope there will be many members contributing 1d. a week or more.

GAYTON THORPE & EAST WALTON

The sum of £13/5/2 was paid into the Penny Club last year, the interest was £3/6/6 making a total of £16/11/8, which was paid out at the beginning of January.

CASTLE RISING & ROYDON

The unhappy dilemma in which the farmers and labourers are involved, owing to fickle politicians who deceived their victims with rosy promises of future prosperity which they have deliberately falsified; coupled with two bad seasons, has landed the agricultural industry in a sorry plight. Masters and men are at loggerheads over a question of wages and hours. Nothing has been settled as we go to press. But by the time this is in your hands it is hoped that an agreement will have been reached. It is always darkest before the dawn.

HILLINGTON

The Flitcham and Hillinton Women's Institute met at the "ffolkes Arms" Barn on 10th of May and heard an interesting lecture on Egypt.

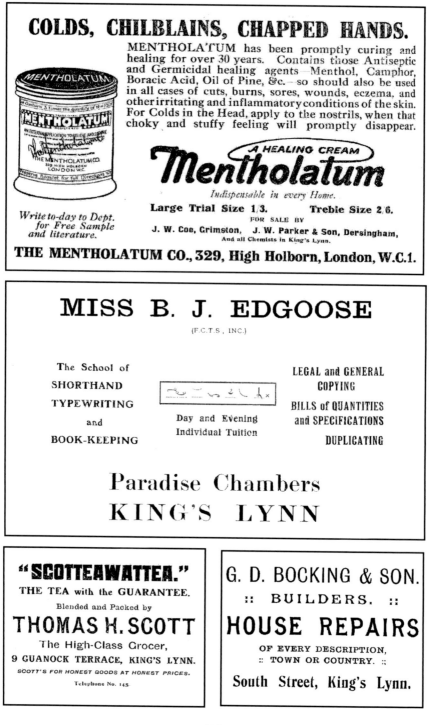

PARISH MAGAZINE.
1923-1924

HILLINGTON

Delegates from the neighbouring Farm Strikers asked for a special service to be held at Hillington Church in the interests of a peaceful settlement in the agricultural dispute. There was a large attendance on the morning of Sunday the 15th.

WOLFERTON & BABINGLEY

Her Royal Highness Princess Mary kindly sent a piece of Christening cake for each of the school children.

WEST WINCH

I regret to say the School is very badly in need of repair and we hope we may be able to have a Sale of Work during the Summer to provide the funds necessary. The amount required will be about £40. His Majesty's Inspector has visited the school and intimated two or three things that require immediate attention.

Unfortunately the managers have not got the funds. If we want to keep the school the money must be found.

HILLINGTON

The Rector wishes it to be known that from henceforth the chairs belonging to the Church will not be available for any entertainments whatever, whether in connection with raising money for Church purposes or not; as considerable damage is done in constant moving. It is useless to improve the Church in one way to make it shabby in another.

GRIMSTON

THINGS OLD. - In the year 1381 a tax was levied throughout the country by which every person was required to pay three groats, that is, a shilling. This was a serious burden; for a man and his wife had to pay six groats, a sum equivalent to a man's wages for a week.

1924

Unfortunately 1924 was not a good year for stories. Most were local births, marriages and deaths, village fetes, choir treats, whist drives, etc. We have already documented the interesting ones in earlier years, but there was one worth including (see below), and plenty of adverts to choose from, so we have used some of these plus a fascinating story from the past. Ed.

GAYTON THORPE & EAST WALTON

On 22nd January, we had the 'Pictures' at the school. There was a full house, and all were sorry to hear that, as the Cinematograph has been sold, it was the last of these entertainments.

GRIMSTON

THINGS OLD. - THE BLACK DEATH 1348-49. It is thought that the general loss in our neighbourhood may well have been half the population. The results of the pestilence were immeasurably great. There were countless widows and orphans. There were men who lost all their relatives. Entire families were blotted out. Crops were left to rot. Cattle were left to starve. The Church was seriously crippled, and education suffered in all its stages. Yet the pestilence became the channel of blessing. It produced a state of society which hastened the departure of the Feudal Ages, and heralded the coming of a new and better social order.

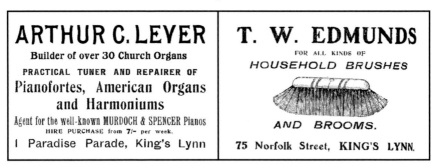

PARISH MAGAZINE.
1925

ASHWICKEN

GIRLS' FRIENDLY SOCIETY

Wednesday, 13th May, will be a day long to be remembered by all the members of the G.F.S. in our Diocese.

It was the day of celebration of the Jubilee of that great society which for 50 years has carried on a splendid work both for the temporal and spiritual benefit of our girls and in these days when the allurements and attractions of the world are so numerous and enticing, it is a matter for deep thankfulness that in the G.F.S. we have a Society which puts the spiritual welfare of its members in the first place. As regards our own parish, 7 members of our branch accompanied by their Associate, Miss Howse and the Rector, attended the great gathering of nearly 3000 at Norwich.

The journey to Norwich was made by means of a Motor Char-a-banc; and a most enjoyable ride it was. Upon our arrival, a celebration of Holy Communion was held in the Church of St. Peter Mancroft, succeeded after lunch by a procession through the streets of the city to the Market Place, where an address of welcome was given by the Lord Mayor, at the conclusion of which a move was made for the Cathedral, where a thanksgiving service was held. The noble building was packed.

CASTLE RISING & ROYDON

G.F.S. JUBILEE DAY AT NORWICH. - There were 174 members present from the Lynn branch 157 going by motor bus, some starting as early as 8 a.m. from King's Lynn and arriving at Norwich at 11.15.

A lovely day made an open air lunch in the Castle Grounds very pleasant, and showed to the full advantage the long, procession of between 2,000 and 3,000 through the streets of Norwich, with the many gay banners of the Branches.

WOLFERTON & BABINGLEY

THE EGGS. 280 eggs were collected from Wolferton and sent through to the Lynn Hospital. Parishioners from Babingley contributed 150 eggs for the Hospital.

CASTLE RISING & ROYDON

The excessive motor traffic passing close by Castle Rising Church on Sunday evenings during the summer months, causes so much disturbance and distraction, that it has been found advisable to transfer the 6.30 p.m, service to the comparative peace and quiet at Roydon, where it is much appreciated.

PARISH MAGAZINE.
1925

NORTH WOOTTON

North Wootton contributed 616 eggs to the recent egg collection for the West Norfolk and King's Lynn Hospital.

GRIMSTON

During some of the most beautiful of Summer days the hand of the great reaper has been three times laid upon members of our community.

Until disabilities prevented her, Mrs. Osborne was amongst the most regular in her attendance at the services of the parish Church. Her end came with great suddenness. May she rest in peace.

A poem beloved of many, a great favourite with President Lincoln, and a great favourite also with a Russian Emperor, has among it stanzas the one following:

> The leaves of the oak
> And the willow shall fade.
> Be scattered around,
> And together be laid;
> And the young and the old,
> And the low and the high,
> Shall moulder to dust,
> And together shall lie.

So it is - young and old, low and high, shall pass away, and their place among us shall know them no more.

HILLINGTON

The Choir outing took place in very delightful weather on 18th July. A large party went to Yarmouth by char-a-banc, where they had dinner and tea and enjoyed themselves in various ways. Expenses on the day were:

Char-a-banc £8/10
Dinners and teas £3/18/3
Refreshments 10/-

A Conservative Fete was held at the Hall on the 25th of July and was largely attended. Viscountess Downe presided at the meeting in the evening, also gave away the various competition prizes etc. It was a very hot and beautiful day and much enjoyed by all.

NORTH RUNCTON & SETCH

Our Choir outing this year was a particular happy and successful one at Hunstanton.

The Sunday school children at Setch also thoroughly enjoyed their visit. Thirty-one children were present and with parents and friends we were a party of between seventy and eighty.

A special feature of the day was the picnic on the beach for the children, when over 120 ham sandwiches disappeared in a marvellous way, though it is not really surprising for they were so good.

PARISH MAGAZINE.
1925-1926

WOLFERTON & BABINGLEY

The Rector is going to act as Chaplain in Italy for six months and Mr Saward has his address. The duty will be taken at Wolferton by a resident Clergyman.

EDITORIAL.

THE LATE QUEEN ALEXANDRA.

The message sent to listeners in, on the wireless on the evening of the 20th November, by the Rev. Archibald Fleming, D.D., will express the sentiments of our readers. For the benefit of those who did not hear it, it is printed below.

Doctor Fleming said, on behalf of the mourning millions, it was desired simply to express their heartfelt sympathy with the King and Queen and the members of the Royal Family in the immeasurable loss that they had sustained in the death of the Queen Mother. Truly all the people of this nation had known her as Queen and as mother; their joys were hers and their sorrows wrung her tender heart...

NORTH RUNCTON & SETCH

The death of Queen Alexandra has called forth world wide expressions of sympathy and sorrow, showing what a wonderful hold she had over the affection of everybody. She has added one more to the blessed memories which England is privileged to cherish and keep fresh of God's women who have gone about doing good, with that Love that "seeketh not her own."

1926

CASTLE RISING & ROYDON
MANOR COURT
AT CASTLE RISING.
Revival of Ancient Customs.

After having been allowed to lapse for more than half a century, the ancient Court Leet and view of Frankpledge with the General Court Baron and Customary Court of Colonel Charles Alfred Howard, D.S.O., Lord of Manor and Leet of Castle Rising, was revived on Wednesday, when it was held at the Black Horse Inn, Castle Rising, before Mr. Harry Lawrence Bradfer-Lawrence, Gentleman, Chief Steward.

Considerable interest was taken in the revival, as no such court had been held since 22nd April, 1874; the court before that took place on 25th February, 1835, and prior to that was held, annually. Frankpledge is "the surety for freemen" and in ancient days the freemen of the Manor were "viewed" from time to time by the

1926

Lord of the Manor for them to pledge themselves for their good behaviour, and that of the other tenants, and for whatever services were due to the King. The latter, of course, in Norman times included fighting.

On Wednesday the old Court Rolls of the Manor were produced, dating from 1642. It is not known where the earlier Rolls are, but it is believed that they are in the possession of the Duke of Norfolk, either at Arundel Castle, or at Norfolk House, London.

Over 40 tenants of the Manor attended and the Lord of the Manor, together with Mr. Bradfer-Lawrence, who was responsible for the revival of the old ceremony, was also present.

The Lord of the Manor, in a brief statement to the Court, welcomed the tenants and explained that the reason for calling the Court was to deal with irregularities and encroachments concerning the commons of the Manor...

The steward then charged the jury. He used the ancient form, explained the various crimes which the court formerly had power to deal and the bailiff made the proclamations: Oyes, Oyes, Oyes. If any person or persons can inform this Court or Inquest of any treasons, felonies, bloodsheds, or any other matters or thing now given in charge, let them come in and they shall be heard...

The business over the bailiff dismissed the Court thus: "Oyes, Oyes, Oyes. All manner of persons have appeared here this day, His majesty's Court Leet and Court Baron of Colonel Charles Alfred Howard, have licence to depart, keeping their day and hour on new summons. God save the King, the Lord of the Manor and the Steward here present."

Afterwards the Lord of the Manor entertained the tenants to dinner.

GRIMSTON

Owing to the Strike no sufficient account of the Concert at Pott Row has appeared in the papers. A long and varied programme was provided by the school children, over 100 scholars appearing on the platform in one capacity or another. So large was the demand for tickets that the concert given first on Wednesday, 21st April, was repeated on Friday the 23rd.

NORTH & SOUTH WOOTTON

Owing to the indisposition of Rector no news has been received from North and South Wootton.

NORTH RUNCTON & SETCH

It was with intense relief and an inward feeling of thankfulness to Almighty God that we heard of the General Strike being called off and it was with our lighter hearts that we approached and kept our Whitsuntide. In spite of the suffering and hardship, which I fear is pressing on many innocent victims of the industrial unrest, we may yet see tokens of Our Lord's promise, " I will not leave you comfortless: I will come unto you."

The temper and fortitude of England is again being sorely tried.

What we must work and prey for is a lasting peace. A peace that will surely come to all that are at peace with God. We must be at peace with one another.

WOLFERTON & BABINGLEY

His Majesty The King has graciously presented a large and very beautiful picture (possibly a copy of a Corregio) "of the Christ" to Wolferton Church, where it is now placed beneath the fine East Window, in front of the High Alter, and it is greatly admired for its beauty.

LITTLE MASSINGHAM

Michaelmas has again arrived and brought with it family departures and comings with corresponding emotions and greetings of farewell and welcome in our village; we have said regretfully goodbye to Broadwaters, Hazels, M. Crows, Parkers and Smiths and now offer our assurance of goodwill to the families of Brighty, Bond, Middleditch and Yull who have already taken possession of the vacated houses.

PARISH MAGAZINE.
1927-1928

APOLOGY FROM THE PRINTER

The Printers beg to solicit the indulgence of their customers of the Parish Magazine for being behind with the publication this month. In addition to some copy reaching them very late, the prevailing epidemic is taking its toll amongst staff.

NORTH RUNCTON & SETCH

I would like to express my sincere sympathy with all the suffers from influenza, and other ailments, with earnest hope for there complete recovery.

GRIMSTON

With great reluctance it has been decided to postpone the choir treats. This is due to members of the choirs who may be ill, and to others who might suffer if the treats were held during the present period.

NORTH & SOUTH WOOTTON

The winter has taken its toll of us in the removal of old parishioners, whose release from the burden of old age is a cause for thankfulness.

NORTH RUNCTON & SETCH

Please excuse my writing much in the way of Parish News. Our great loss is hard to bear and we have joined a large circle where all hearts beat as one and the sympathy, spoken and unspoken which we know is felt for us is a great help. We too think of others who suffer losses more terrible than ours. Our dear boy fell from a bastion while ashore at Malta.

He is buried in the Naval Cemetery there. We hope to have a small Tablet to his memory in our Church here.

I remain your very sincere Friend and Rector,

E. M. PLUMPTRE.

WOLFERTON & BABINGLEY

London holiday children, have found kind friends in the village who have taken them in for a fortnight's holiday. Mrs. Batterbee had four boys, Mrs. Bell two girls, Mrs. W. Godfrey two girls and Mrs. Dan Batterbee two girls, ten children in all.

1928

GRIMSTON

Very severe weather has marked the Christmas season. Not for a score of years has the cold been so sharp. Christmas

Day services suffered in consequence. But the Church looked very sweet in its decorations, carried out by the customary helpers, though in the absence of the Rector, suffering from a cold.

CONGHAM

The Congham Widows desire to thank Captain Elwes, Sir Evard ffolkes, Mr W. F. Marshall, Rev. S. R. & Mrs. Kersley for their Christmas gifts.

NORTH RUNCTON & SETCH

We were all, I am sure, very sorry indeed to hear about the serious accident to Charlie Goss, who has had the misfortune of having had both his legs and arms broken, while engaged in some work of which the scaffolding gave way.

WOLFERTON & BABINGLEY

S.P.G. – A most interesting Lantern Lecture on China was given on Friday 10th February, in the Pavilion by Rev. H. Mathews, who has recently returned home after years' service in China at Shantung.

Some splendid scenes of the life and architecture of China were portrayed and a picture was given of a young Clergyman who had gone out to work with Mr. Mathews, and who was foully murdered soon after his arrival.

GRIMSTON

Among matters discussed by the Church Council there were several connected with the Churchyard. In order to secure a thorough understanding of the facts, a Committee of Enquiry was appointed.

It is perhaps not generally known that three of our former members of Grimston choir are now organists in neighbouring Parishes.

Mr. Osborne at Congham, Mrs. Petch at Hillington, and Mrs. A. Phillippo at Roydon.

Every Sunday in fact our Parish provides five organists in all. It is only fair to add that we must to a considerable extent attribute this to the labours and influence of our former organist, Mrs. Hammond.

Among the last twenty-five burials in our Churchyard only five were those of persons under sixty, and only three of persons under fifty. On the other hand one was over ninety, seven others were over eighty, six others were over seventy, and six others over sixty. The average age indeed was as high as sixty-six.

If we take all the burials in the year 1828, we find the average

age was only twenty-seven. There were nineteen burials in the year, and of the nineteen persons buried, only one reached the age of eighty, only one was registered among the seventies, none in the sixties, and none in the fifties. But seven were under two, two were in the "Teens," and two in the twenties.

In the matter of Physical health the lives of men have been revolutionized. The improvement has come about through the labours of a comparatively small number of men working on scientific lines.

ASHWICKEN

At the PCC meeting the question arose as to the future of the Nursing Fund, and after discussion it was unanimously resolved that it should be closed and that no further subscriptions should be asked for and no further grants made.

CASTLE RISING & ROYDON

The motor season is now in full swing again, the cars that pass through Castle Rising on a Sunday are counted by thousands. Lest this passing pageant of movement should so fascinate any of our Parishioners, that they are tempted in consequence to withhold their help from the work of God's Church, without which

help that work must fail, let them be warned in time, and by their example at any rate bear witness Sunday by Sunday to their Faith.

LITTLE MASSINGHAM

Col. and Lady Joan Birkbeck received a warm welcome upon their return from their honeymoon. On the arrival of their motor car at the Lodge, an enthusiastic team of workers on the estate attached ropes to it and preceded by the Massingham band and attended by a crowd of local well-wishers, they were brought to the door of their home.

CASTLE RISING & ROYDON

HISTORICAL DISJECTA MEMBRA.

Below is an extract from an old will expressing the wishes of a former parishioner. Date unknown. Ed.

JOHN CLERK of Northwotton, yeoman.

To be buried in the South side of the churchyard of All Saints in Northwotton. I will have at either end of my grave two substantial crosses of timber set and scripture made upon either cross for a remembrance, to the intent that those who see or read the scripture shall pray for my soul.

PARISH MAGAZINE.
1928-1929

WEST WINCH

The schools examination in Religious Knowledge was taken by the Rev. Douglas Smith, Diocesan Inspector. He reports as follows:- "Throughout the School the Plastercine Modelling is excellent. I wish more Schools used this method of impressing Bible stories etc., upon the minds of children."

LITTLE MASSINGHAM

The Commission appointed to report to the Bishop upon the desirability of uniting the benefices of Great and Little Massingham, held a public enquiry in Great Massingham Village Hall. There was a large attendance, and it was evident that those present were almost unanimously opposed to the suggested union.

The Rector received 60 men of the parish as his guests at the Rectory, on New Years Eve, when a very pleasant evening was spent, and concluded with the National Anthem, and Big Ben on the wireless.

CASTLE RISING & ROYDON

NURSING ASSOCIATION.- The Secretary wishes to point out that if the District desires to retain Nurse Barber, every effort must be made to support the Fund.

CONGHAM

THE CHURCH. - Gramophone services were held in the parish church on 30th December and 6th January during the afternoon. At the beginning, there were short evening services with hymns. The programme included: Carols by the Westminster Choir and "Ave Maria" sung by John McCormack. The collections were for the Choir Fund and Miner's Distress Fund.

GRIMSTON

The collections on behalf of the Coalfields Distress Funds made on the last Sunday of 1928, amounted to £3/3/0, and the collection earlier in the month on behalf of the C.M.S., amounted to £1/7/8.

GAYTON THORPE & EAST WALTON

The death of William Alcock on Sunday night 17th February has removed a familiar figure from the parish. The whole of his life has been spent in Gayton Thorpe and he was born, lived and has died in the same house.

In spite of being deaf and dumb those who knew him well found no great difficulty in conversing with him. We shall all miss "Dummy" as he was generally called, for he was everybody's favourite. It is interesting to note

PARISH MAGAZINE.
1929

that he and his forbears have been at Gayton Thorpe for over 200 years. The first person of his name entered in the Registers being John Alcock, who died in 1711, and is stated to have been "buried in sheep's wool only" according to law.

GRIMSTON

A bit of Ancient Grimston, the Old Bell Inn, has just disappeared, raising clouds of dust and greater clouds of suspicion, for in the course of their operations, the workmen discovered some human remains.

It is said that about twenty years ago, other human remains were discovered on the ground attached to the Inn, and there are stories that at an earlier date there were similar discoveries in the grounds connected with the Paddox and at the Brewery.

It is not necessary to imagine there has been foul play, though to many people the connection with an Inn seems at least suggestive. Perhaps in some or all of the instances that are mentioned, the explanation will be provided by the Black Death, when many of the victims were hurriedly burned without the rites of the Church, and close to the place where they died.

Photo of the Bell Inn on page 115

WEST WINCH

The Rural Dean on his visit to the Church noticed the large cracks in the Church Tower and one of the pinnacles standing at a dangerous angle. He advised that it should be attended to as soon as possible.

The work was given to J. J. Bone and Son, Lynn, and we are pleased to say is now completed. The cost will be somewhere about £35 or £40, and will be paid from the money raised by fetes for the Church Restoration Fund.

GRIMSTON

In the notes on the Bell Inn in the June Magazine there were several errors and one of them requires correction. A reference is made that the victims of the Black Death as being "hurriedly burned". This should have read "hurriedly buried".

ASHWICKEN

SCHOOL NEWS. - A meeting of Managers was held on Friday, 5th July, at which the estimate, for the cost of laying on water from the Lynn Corporation was presented, and it was agreed that should this estimate be inclusive of all cost, it should be accepted. This of course was subject to obtaining the consent of the Lynn Water Works Committee to tap their main.

The Bell Inn 1910 *(Rev. W. Howard)*

Walnut Farm and Grimston clock 1934 *(Rev. W. Howard)*

Grimston Old Rectory 1910 *(Rev. W. Howard)*

The Limes, South Wootton *(Jeanne Fox)*

The Rev. Kersley and the Congham choir *(David Grimes)*

Box Pews in East Walton Church *(Bill Lewis)*

Village sign *(Bill Lewis)*

Wheelwright's oven *(Bill Lewis)*

Inside the
wheelwright's oven *(Bill Lewis)*

Rare three tier pulpit
in East Walton church *(Bill Lewis)*

PARISH MAGAZINE.

1929

GAYTON THORPE & EAST WALTON

As Chairman of the Parish Meeting at East Walton, I have been notified officially that the office of Parish Constable will cease to exist after 24th March, 1930.

Overseers dating back to 1601 were abolished in 1927. Guardians of the Poor have received their death blow. One wonders who are next on the list to be abolished;- let us hope that it will be Tax Inspectors and Collectors.

The Parish Constable, formerly known as the Tythingman, held an important position. In past days Local Manor Courts carried out work now done by Magistrates, County Court Judges, County and District Councillors: and when the Court Leet *i.e.* the Court dealing with crime and offence, was opened, it was the business of the Court to make enquiry as to "how the Constable or Tythingman has discharged his duties in arresting felons, raising hue and cry in cases of murder, violence, etc."

The Court also made enquiries as to the "condition of the Parish Stocks, the Tythingman's prison." The Tythingman had also to report if any path to "Church, Mill or Market" had been stopped up, or any wrong enclosures made.

Parish Stocks, in which unruly persons were placed by the Constable to cool their heels, are things of the past.

The Constable himself is now in the melting pot, and I, for one, am sorry that this ancient and honourable Office, which dates back to Saxon times, is being abolished.

A.R.V.D.

ASHWICKEN

SCHOOL NEWS. – The laying on of drinking water for the use of our children is now a fact. It only remains now for us to pay the cost of it. We have in hand £22/2/0 and hope our other parishioners will enable us to provide the balance.

GAYTON THORPE & EAST WALTON

On several of the tombstones at East Walton is the sacred monogram I.H.S., and there seems to be some doubt as to the actual meaning of these letters, for quite recently I have heard them explained as signifying "In His Steps." Other explanations sometimes given are "I Have Suffered," and *"Jesus Hominum Salvator"* i.e. "Jesus Saviour of men." Though beautiful in their way, these explanations are not correct. I.H.S. is the abbreviated form of the Holy Name JESUS in Greek. In the catacombs at Rome,

PARISH MAGAZINE.
1929-1930

where Christians buried their dead during the terrible persecutions which raged from A.D. 64 to A.D. 303, the monogram commonly used was X.P., the first two letters of the name CHRIST in Greek; and when placed over a grave signified "In Christ" or "Asleep in Christ," and so I.H.S. on a tombstone signifies that the person buried is asleep "In Jesus".

THINGS OLD. - In 1695 an Act came into force placing a tax on windows, which practically meant that people were taxed for allowing the light of the sun to shine in at their windows; no doubt it was the Daylight Saving Bill of those enlightened times. More peculiar still was the Act of 1667, Ordering Burial in Woollen; and as it was evaded on every possible occasion, a more stringent Act was passed in 1678. Not only must the dead be wrapped in woollen, but the Act ordered that even "the quilling round the inside of any coffin and the ligature round the feet of the corpse" be woollen also.

The Act for burying in woollen was passed for the lessening the importation of linen from beyond seas, and for the encouragement of the woollen and paper manufactures of this Kingdom. It gradually fell into disuse and eventually was repealed.

A.R.V.D.

1930

GAYTON THORPE & EAST WALTON

Due to a shortage of interesting parish news for this year, we are capitalising on this Rector's historical research. As these articles make fascinating reading, we are including several of them. Ed.

At West Bilney, an adjoining parish, is this entry in the registers:

"1590, A nurse child was buried the 18th October."

In parishes near London, and sometimes near large towns like Norwich, the burial of nurse children was by no means uncommon.

Townspeople who had sufficient means, put their children out to nurse in the country for the sake, it was said, of fresh air. But that so many of these nurse children died and were buried unnamed, leads one to suppose that, for obvious reasons, they were not wanted and so were placed with people who made a livelihood by baby-farming.

Apparently it was no difficult matter to dispose of an infant; even the Foundling Hospital, built in 1739, did little to stop the terrible loss of child life. During the first four years of its existence, 14,934 infants were

119

PARISH MAGAZINE.
1930

admitted, and it is stated that not more than 4000 of them survived.

If correct, these figures are appalling. Perhaps this helps to explain why the English are such a hardy race of people; it is a case of survival of the fittest.

Fortunately for us, some children simply would not die, but insisted on living and growing up to man's estate.

A.R.V.D

HISTORICAL NOTE

Headstones and coffins seem to have come into general use about the same time, for coffined burial was not usual until 1700 or even later.

A well-known Judge once pointed out that a parishioner had "a naked right of burial in his parish churchyard, but it was not clear whether he had a right to bury a big box as well." The Prayer Book provides for the burial of the Corpse only. The Priest is to meet the Corpse at the gate. At the grave the Corpse is to be made ready. At the Committal, earth is to be cast on the Body.

At South Wootton Church, unless I am mistaken, can still be seen the old Hearse with the Parish Shell, in which the dead were placed and brought to the Church for burial. Coffined burial does not seem to have met with general approval, and coffins were spoken of rather scornfully,

as wooden Josephs, owing, I suppose, to Joseph being "put in a coffin in Egypt."

A.R.V.D.

An interesting piece of history. John or as he was sometimes called Thomas Rolfe was born and baptised in Narford: who afterwards married the red American Indian Princess Pocahontas, and brought her to England in the reign of James I.

Pocahontas was daughter to Powhatan, Emperor of Virginia, and was also known as Matoaka. It said that John Rolfe was the first settler in Virginia "to whom it occurred to grow tobacco for the English Market and his enterprise, although less well-known was as important as the achievement of Sir Walter Raleigh, who first set an example of the use of it."

Most of us in the parish - I speak of course for the male portion only - enjoy an occasional Virginia Cigarette, but probably few are aware how greatly they are indebted for this mild and inexpensive luxury, to a Norfolk man and a neighbour.

A.R.V.D.

Sir William Barkham did not die at East Walton Hall, but at his London residence in Great Kirby Street, Hatton Garden. He describes himself in his Will, as 'Sick in body but of sound and perfect memory.'...

His Will however, although admitted to probate, was never actually signed. What happened was this:-

Robert Walpole, of Houghton, called at Great Kirby Street on Saturday, 21st December, 1695, and found Sir William Barkham ill in bed.

Knowing that no Will had been made, he urged Sir William to do so, and Thomas Gilbert, a scrivener, was then and there called in, who wrote out the Will on three sheets of paper.

Sir William with very little assistance then sat up in bed, and a pen was placed in his hand, but before he could sign his name he became unconscious, and died three hours later.

A.R.V.D.

NORTH RUNCTON, SETCH AND HARDWICK

I hope that the Hospital Contributory Scheme, which has just been started, will be well supported. I think it will, for we all know what a great work is done by the Hospitals for the relief of suffering.

The minimum amount asked for, is a penny a week, but those who can afford it, may give more. The payment covers husband, wife, and children under the age of 16, and entitles them to Hospital treatment free of charge, for a period of eight weeks.

No contributor may claim this privilege until after eight weeks contribution. Mrs. Rounce will visit every house that contributes once a fortnight, or once a month.

PARISH MAGAZINE.
1931

WOLFERTON & BABINGLEY

It was with very deep regret that we learned of the death of Mr Rice. Rector of Wolferton – an office which he held for 17 years (1912 to 1928)...

HILLINGTON

The employees on the Hillington Estate wish to express their grateful thanks to Viscountess Downe for beef at Christmas.

LITTLE MASSINGHAM

The Judgement of the Lords of the Judicial Committee of the Privy Council in the matter of the Union of the Benefices of Great and Little Massingham, delivered on the 23rd February, 1931, has lifted a heavy cloud which has been hanging threateningly over our parish for two-and-a-half years.

The unity and independence which the parish has enjoyed for centuries, its possession of a Rectory and a Rector of its own, seemed in danger of being taken away from it for ever. Now we know that these will be permanently retained.

GAYTON THORPE & EAST WALTON

Judging by a remark made, some appear to think that a parson has less work to occupy his time than other people. But is this really so? I myself have had various experiences in life, at one time serving as an N.C.O. in a battalion of Foot Guards; and it was easier for me to do a twenty-four hours guard on Buckingham Palace with a picket thrown in, than it is to prepare two sermons for an ordinary Sunday's Duty.

Nothing to my mind is more difficult than producing, week after week, two sermons which will be of interest, as one hopes, and of help. Most people do not give their parsons sufficient credit for the hours spent over books and commentaries each week, otherwise I feel sure there would be more present at the Sunday Services to hear him preach.

CASTLE RISING & ROYDON

Congratulations to Mrs. Ashton, who attained her one hundred and second birthday on Whit-Sunday, 24th May. She was honoured by a visit from their Majesties The King and Queen and His Grace the Archbishop of Canterbury, on Whit-Monday.

PARISH MAGAZINE.
1931-1932

NORTH RUNCTON, SETCH AND HARDWICK

The recent earthquake has not left much impression behind, chiefly because there are no visible signs that there has been any such thing: some slept through it, others were startled if not alarmed.

How thankful we ought to be that no lives were lost and no damage was done. At the same time we may well ask if it is not one way in which God is speaking to us to rouse and awaken us to a sense of the great need there is in these days of repentance and turning to Him.

CASTLE RISING & ROYDON

THE LODGE FARM. - Capt. A. Knight very much regrets having to vacate his farm, owing to agricultural depression, which has been held by his family for three generations since 1850.

Sympathetic interest has been taken in the sales of household furniture, agricultural implements, and stock, which took place on 23rd and 25th Sept. respectively. Capt. Knight has been Church-warden of the Parish Church for the past seven years.

GRIMSTON

Politics have engaged the attention of many of our number, and even as I write, people are casting their votes. By the time this is in print a new Government will have been elected, but our duty in the affairs of our nation will not have ended, for we should ever pray for those who are elected that God may bestow on them the spirit of wisdom and of true religion, so that our nation may be brought safely through these critical times.

1932

HILLINGTON

Wireless Services from Westminster Abbey and York Minster have been very successfully broadcasted in the Church weekly during Lent.

NORTH RUNCTON, SETCH AND HARDWICK

I am afraid we are apt to be a bit late sometimes in beginning the 11 o'clock Service on Sunday mornings. This is principally due to the fact that it is rather a rush for me to get back from Sunday School at Setch, even with a car. To rush into Church at the last minute is hardly the thing to do, and is really disrespectful to God, and is a poor preliminary to worship. I will try and mend my ways, and I hope that no one will rely on my being a minute or two late.

NORTH & SOUTH WOOTTON

A very pleasant social gathering took place at North Wootton, for the purpose of recognizing the services of Mr. J. Shipp in the parish, during more than 44 years of his Church-wardenship. The Rector on behalf of the many parishioners and others, asked Mr. Shipp to accept an Electric Wireless Set as an expression of his services to the parish.

GRIMSTON

There was a Meeting of the Parochial Church Council on Friday the 5th August. It had been especially called to consider the heating of the Church. Everyone agrees it is unsatisfactory and the matter has become urgent.

The Rector had been asked to find out what he could, about the McClary (pipeless) system. While on holiday he had visited two Churches where this had been in use. In both cases it had been a complete success. A resolution was moved and carried that an estimate be obtained for installing the McClary system in the Parish Church.

FLITCHAM

The Choir and Bell-Ringers' Outing to Yarmouth on 3rd August, was most enjoyable. One of our number seemed to find that part of Norfolk so enticing that he has only just returned!

NORTH RUNCTON, SETCH AND HARDWICK

To save the managers the expense, Miss Linton has very kindly spent part of her holiday in distempering the walls of the two School classrooms, and we are very grateful to her.

126

CASTLE RISING & ROYDON

TRINITY HOSPITAL. – Her Majesty the Queen very graciously gave a Christmas dinner to the governess and sisters on 29th December. Beautiful flowers from the Royal Gardens adorned the table. The sumptuous repast was greatly enjoyed.

WEST WINCH

The Heating Apparatus has been renewed but the first two Sundays it was used it did not give good results, doubtless because we do not yet know the best way of using it.

Since the days when our Churchyards were planted with yew, to furnish the best bows for Archers, shooting has always been a national sport, and it is therefore with much pleasure that we congratulate Mrs. Archdale on the success of her eldest son, Lt. C. Archdale of the 1st Manchester Regiment, who at the age of 29 has won the cup for the rifle championship for the Army.

CASTLE RISING & ROYDON

Owing to the agricultural depression and the introduction of the motor, many country blacksmiths find their occupation somewhat curtailed, and have to turn their hands to other ways of earning a livelihood. This is the case with Mr. F. E. Colman, our blacksmith at Castle Rising, who has added chimney sweeping to his ordinary trade. We wish him success in his enterprise.

At the end of September, a mild sensation was caused by Leslie Pointer, who, while digging in his father's garden, unearthed a skeleton. As far as could be ascertained it was that of a child about ten to twelve years old. The teeth were in perfect condition, but the leg bones were missing. Speculation is ripe as to how and when the child came to be buried there. No local tradition is known which might offer some explanation, and the mystery still remains unsolved.

The final article! It proves how best laid plans can be changed to go in a different direction! Ed.

GRIMSTON

Eighteen members of our Church Council visited Colkirk and Narborough Churches by car. The Rectors met us and were most kind in explaining the electric lighting. We liked the story of the Narborough gentleman who was buried in a raised tomb and in an upright position, lest he should be trodden on, but whose bones were at a later date removed and placed under a seat at the end of the Church, with the result that he is now repeatedly sat upon!

A few additional interesting photographs

An early photo of the former Lynn Arms at Setch   *(David Apps)*

(Maggie & Roger Haverson)

Villagers leaving Anmer in 1936 to pay their respects at Sandringham as the body of King George V was taken to London

Children outside Anmer Post Office c1930

(Maggie & Roger Haverson)

Congham High House- date unknown

(Rev. W. Howard)

Grimston Road railway station in its heyday- date unknown

(Rev.W. Howard)

Finally, a few articles that appeared at the end of the 1908-10 Parish Magazines from the 'Home Words' company.

An Unusual Belfry

The following incident occurred in the village of Stanton, Suffolk. On March 5, 1906, a low rumbling noise was heard by the parishioners, and they discovered that the tower of All Saints' Church had fallen, together with the clock and belfry of five bells, valued at £800.

The debris was cleared and services resumed in the church on Easter Sunday following, minus the ringing of the bells, much to the regret of the parish clerk, who thereupon thought of a device for calling the worshippers to service, by having a bell arranged between the branches of a tree growing in the churchyard, and as there were no funds for the rebuilding of the tower, it still continues doing its duty there. There were previous signs of dilapidation, and only the day before the fall both Dean and Rector were up in the Tower and only fifteen minutes before it fell the clerk wound up the clock in the belfry.

A Useful Ambulance

The Rev. Cecil White, Vicar of St. Peter's, Hornsey, a few months ago opened an ambulance station at the corner of Turnpike Lane, Hornsey, N. It has been erected and equipped by funds resulting from a concert organized by a local resident, and voluntary gifts collected in his off-duty time by P. C. Newman, who is seen standing beside the Ambulance

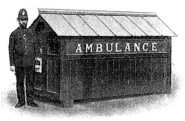

Station. After speaking of the value of "First Aid" the Rev. Cecil White said that he had been informed that the ambulance could be used for the removal of bed-ridden persons on their changing residence, either gratuitously or on payment of a very small charge. The local members of the St. John's Ambulance Association are anxious that this enterprise should be followed in other quarters where no such conveniences exist.

 Parishioners of Bratton in Wilts have been engaged in an unusual form of work. Desirous of having gas in their church, but finding the expense too high, they solved the difficulty in a very practical manner. The church was about a quarter of a mile from the nearest gas main, and it was necessary that a trench should be dug this distance before a supply of gas could be laid to the church. The vicar called for volunteers to do the work and with pick and spade and shovel they worked "like navvies". So in this remote country church the services can now be held in a light such as many a town church might envy.

In a village near Newcastle a miner's wife presented him with twins. In the usual time the twins had to he christened, and George, his wife and his friends proceeded to church. The clergyman asked the father the names of the children, and he quite proudly replied, "Steak and Kidney, sor." "Come, come," replied the clergyman. "These are odd names for your children," when the indignant wife interrupted "What d'ye mean, Geordie? Its Kate and Sidney." "Ay, it is, sor! Aa thout it was like summit to eat!" murmured George.

The owner of a property near to Tattingstone wished to have a church included in the view from his house. So he built a skeleton church onto a cottage, the result being that from *his* point of view a  church is seen, and from the opposite side an unusual cottage.

A generation ago, in the churchyard of Selmeston, Sussex, there was a tombstone remarkable for its size. An elaborate inscription covered the whole surface of the stone. The departed was described as a model husband and father, but no one was buried there. In the centre of a capital "O" in the inscription was a knob, which would escape the observation of all but those who expected to find it. On turning this knob continuously the stone rose on hinges until it was upright instead of horizontal. A number of steps descended into a huge vault capable of holding a vast amount of goods. This was one of the hiding places where smugglers hid wine and brandy in large quantities.

An All-Round Country Rector

BY OUR OWN COMMISSIONER.

KNOW everything of something and something of everything is no doubt a counsel of perfection, but Mr. G. T. Altimas Ward, Rector of Eastington, Gloucester, has gone further than most men to realize its worth. As most rectors and vicars have discovered, their parishioners expect them to be men of many parts, and a knowledge of medicine, carpentering, cooking, and even needle-work, has often been found invaluable, as a bishop of our church has more than once testified.

But no one expects such versatility as Mr. Ward has shown. For four years he has been Rector of Eastington, where his zeal and boundless enthusiasm have won for him the esteem and loyalty of his parishioners.

I reached the rectory somewhat earlier than I was expected and found the Rector seated at his organ in the act of revising a setting of "Lead kindly Light," which he had just composed. I should explain that Mr. Ward is an all-round musician, and was once a pupil of the late Sir Robert Prescot Stewart, Professor of Music in the University of Dublin.

When he was a boy, both the harmonium and the piano had to be locked against him, so great was his enthusiasm for music. In his undergraduate days he was the hon. assistant organist at the Chapel of his University, Trinity College, Dublin, and for some time was Precentor of the Parish Church, Kingston Hill, Orpington, and St George's, Catford. He has composed many hymn tunes, chants, kyries, anthems, etc., which have had, and still have, a large circulation. Mr. Ward trains his own choir, and when a stranger occupies the pulpit Mr. Yard himself very often presides at the organ.

Any parishioner who chooses is allowed to attend the weekly choir practice, and many local organists also avail themselves of the privilege; indeed, sometimes there are almost as many at the practices as there are at the regular services on Sunday. The choir practice thus becomes a very real service of praise, at which the utmost reverence prevails.

Eastington possesses a parish brass band, and having said what I have, no one will be surprised to hear that the Rector himself is the conductor of it. He can play any one of the instruments from the big drum upwards.

The Rector has built for himself a complete general printing office, and he has two or three printing presses. He prints his own church music, his own magazine notes, all his parish notices, choir lists, Sunday School registers, lessons, etc. I asked the Rector where he spent his apprenticeship as a compositor. His reply was, "in the school of necessity." He began by trying his hand at printing church music, and his success led him on to more ambitious work. He explained that he considered printing a nearly necessary part of the education of a country clergyman, particularly in parishes where the finances do not admit of the shop-keepers taking up the advertising space in the local magazine and thus helping to make it as nearly self-supporting as possible.

The typewriter too, and its very necessary companion, the duplicator, also form part of the Rector's stock-in-trade, if I may so express it. He is a skilful typist, and, in addition, is a writer of Pitman's shorthand.

Amongst some of his extra parochial occupations, amateur carpentering must not be overlooked. The Rector put up his own workshop, measuring some 25 ft. x 12 ft., and he is contemplating himself erecting a Parish Hall on his glebe land and presenting it to the parish. It will be a wooden structure, match-boarded inside, and will he built on an iron frame with a roof of corrugated iron. If a little woodturning is required the Rector simply takes off his coat and does it at his own lathe.

The Rector of Eastington is one of the most ardent motorists in the county, and he owns four cars. He has motored over Alpine passes, and, indeed, over most of the continent of Europe. He has been a great traveller, having visited Palestine, Egypt, Greece, and a large part of the continents of Asia and Africa.

I questioned the Rector as to the actual use of the motor-car for strictly parochial purposes. "Personally I could not get on without it," he said, "and the more I see of the working of country parishes, and the possibilities of the car, the more I am inclined to think they will eventually revolutionize existing arrangements. For one thing," he said, "it will be possible to unite country parishes and work them by means of the motor-car, particularly those which cover a very large area and are thinly populated." He thinks that the parish motor-car may one day become almost as common as, say, the parish clerk. Mr. Ward constantly obtains the help of outside preachers, and this in many cases would be quite impossible but for the aid of the car, the train service - or rather the lack of it - making the journey in a given time next door to impossible. He frequently motors the Gloucester Bishop to and from his church.

The parish of Eastington, though large, is not scattered, and by the help of this modern means of locomotion, it is possible to get from one end of it to the other in six minutes. The Rector could not do anything like as much moving about as he does were he not an expert motorist.

He is a most considerate driver and totally devoid of sympathy with the "show-off" man at the wheel.

Every now and then Mr. Ward invites the members of the mothers' meeting to a motor-car trip, and himself at the wheel of the leading car, conducts them for a run of sixty, seventy, or even a hundred miles. And the members of the choir are also similarly favoured.

"Are not some of the mothers a little timid of riding in the cars?" I asked. The Rector replied that they had a wonderful confidence in him, although he admitted that he was quite unable to fathom the depths of their hearts as to their actual feelings when the car was going fast.

Mr. Ward does absolutely all his own motor repairs. He vulcanizes his own tyres and turns at his own lathe any particular part that may require replacing.

During the winter months the Rector makes a feature of magic lantern exhibitions. This form of entertainment appeals strongly to the villagers, and the Rector delights to entertain them in this way.

Paraffin lamps still hold sway in the village, but the Rector was dissatisfied with them at the rectory and so he personally fixed up an installation of acetylene gas. So successful was it that it has since been copied in several of the larger houses in the neighbourhood.

Archery and photography are two of the Rector's favourite recreations. He keeps a couple of dogs, and is very fond of them, but his constant companion is a Brazilian parrot which hops about the table and partakes of a little refreshment when his master's eye is otherwise engaged.

Speaking of this parrot, Mr. Ward explained to me that one could never tell what particular sentence would leave an impression on a parrot's mind. "You might," he said, "take infinite pains in trying to teach a parrot to repeat certain words but without success, whereas the bird might catch hold of a stray sentence repeated only once."

One morning Mr. Ward rang for a cup of tea to be brought to his bedroom. Quite casually one servant maid said to the other, "The Rector wants a cup of tea." The parrot heard and remembered the sentence and now frequently gives utterance to it.

The bird has a remarkably good pair of ears. When the Rector is away callers naturally say to the person answering the door, "where is the Rector?" This is another phrase the bird has seized upon and the query, "where is the Rector?"

A glance at the library revealed amongst an array of other books a number of splendid volumes dealing with metaphysics and astronomy - sciences in which the Rector is particularly interested.

An enormous collection of Goss and other china from all parts of the world may be seen in one of the old-fashioned rooms, and the Rector prizes it highly.

Mr. Ward is a bachelor. Some of his intimate friends sometimes darkly hint that it is time he was, so to speak, running in double harness, and even I ventured the remark, "and are you never lonely?" only to receive the answer, "never, in the very last degree; I am much too busy a man." The pathetic little word "lonely" is unknown to him, and he assured me he could not under any circumstances define it from personal experience if asked to do so. His life and methods, if better known by others, would make many an otherwise weary hour pleasanter for the dull, and even more profitable for the worker.

Mr. Ward comes of a literary family and is an excellent linguist. Several valuable books have come from his pen, in addition to his musical compositions.

After all that activity I feel exhausted, perhaps it's time to sign off! Ed.

Contacts

THE CHURCH OF ENGLAND
Diocese of Norwich:
www.norwich.anglican.org/

'THE GREAT GOVERNMENT AERODROME'

This A4, 146 page hardback book, written by David E. Turner and published by the Narborough Airfield Research Group, is packed with fascinating information and pictures about the Narborough Airfield during the first world war.

A few copies are still available from the author.

He can be contacted on 01760 337768.

David E. Turner,
60, Eastfields,
Narborough,
King's Lynn.
PE32 1ST

Lynn Museums:
Market Street,
King's Lynn,
Norfolk.
PE30 1NL
www.museums.norfolk.gov.uk

The Liddle Collection is held at:
Special Collections,
University of Leeds,
Leeds.
LS2 9JT
www.leeds.ac.uk/library/spcoll/

The Castle Rising History Group:
www.castle-rising-history.co.uk

For information about obtainting further copies of this
book please visit our website:
www.newrevelationsbook.co.uk